A Tea for All Seasons

Mary Pielenz Hampton

ZondervanGifts

We have a gift for inspiration™

For all my "tea friends" from seasons
past and seasons yet to come
—Mary Pielenz Hampton

We would appreciate hearing from you. Please send your
comments to us in care of the address below. And be sure to
recommend this product to your friends. Thank you.

ZondervanPublishingHouse
Mail Drop B20
Grand Rapids, Michigan 49530
http://www.zondervan.com

A Tea for all Seasons
Copyright © 1997 by Mary Pielenz Hampton

ISBN 0-310-96912-3

Published in association with the literary agency of Alive Communications, Inc., 1465 Kelly Johnson
Blvd., #320, Colorado Springs, CO 80920

Senior Editor: Joy Marple
Production Editor: Pat Matuszak
Art Design: Cheryl Van Andel

Printed in Mexico

99 /DR/ 3   2

Acknowledgments

Every book requires a unique team to see it through to completion. It was a special joy to work with the team that came together for this time:

My immeasurable appreciation to my husband, Dean, for his tremendous encouragement for my work and patience with the accompanying inconveniences. A heart that has found a home has great capacity for inspiration. I look forward to many more seasons together and am grateful for the inspiration you bring to my life.

Working with Joy Marple and Cheryl Van Andel made creating this book more enjoyable than I expected publishing could be. Thank you for taking my original idea, expanding the vision and including me all along the way. I look forward to our continuing relationship.

There aren't words enough to thank Bob and Katy Davis and their staff at the Apple Farm Inn and Gift Shop in San Luis Obispo. I can't imagine a better location for the photographs or more accommodating staff anywhere. Much of the charm in this book reflects the charm of your business. Thank you for sharing it with us so generously.

Many others contributed to making the finished project so lovely. It was a pleasure to work with Janet Baird at Country Classics, the staff at Forden's and everyone at The Parable, all located in San Luis Obispo. I am fortunate to have lived for so long in a community filled with such generous people.

Many thanks to my former coworkers at the Employment Development Department for your encouragement as I embarked upon this new career and your enthusiastic response to the recipes you sampled for me.

It was a joy to share the developing lessons with the ladies of my "Third Thursday Tea" group. Thanks for the encouragement that comes from knowing that busy women really do desire to spend time with the Lord.

And finally, although it has been said before, "I thank Christ Jesus our Lord who strengthened me, because He considered me faithful, putting me into service." 1 Timothy 1:12 (NASB)

Contents

Introduction

Time and Seasons

There are seasons in nature and seasons in our lives. We even use the word "season" for adding flavor to foods. In the same way that spices add variety to the foods they season, so the seasons bring variety into our lives.

Our early years, like Spring, are a time of budding. Tender hearts and minds learning, building, exploring, maturing. Summer is a season of blossoming. It's the time when proper preparation and nurturing begins to show results. Autumn finds us reaping the fruits of our labor. The abundant harvest is a testimony to all the work that has been done before. Winter is a time of rest. A time to live off the provisions that were stored up from the harvest.

A Tea for All Seasons is for you, in whatever season you find yourself. Together we'll look at times or seasons through which you may have

> *Tea refreshes the body.*
> *Time spent with the Lord*
> *refreshes the soul.*
>
>

already passed. Other pages may discuss a time you have yet to encounter. But wherever you've been, and wherever you may still go, *A Tea for All Seasons* can be a companion throughout every season.

My desire is that this book will help you to see the Lord in both the ordinary and extraordinary moments of your life. I hope that you will discover in a new way that *"Times of refreshing . . . come from the presence of the Lord."* Acts 3:19b (NASB)

Tea refreshes the body. Time spent with the Lord refreshes the soul. *A Tea for All Seasons* brings the two together for a unique experience of refreshment.

Throughout the world teatime is a time set apart from the hurried pace of the day. Just the simple act of putting on the kettle and waiting for the water to boil is an act of slowing down, of pausing, of anticipation.

In some places teatime is a social event. In other places it is a spiritual ceremony. But wherever and however it is observed, teatime involves dedicating a portion of the day to reflection. Perhaps that is why the idea of blending teatime and devotional time seems such a natural union.

At times we come into the Lord's presence together, as part of a congregation at church or in sweet fellowship with a friend. Other times we meet him on our own, at the kitchen table with our Bibles open or sitting in the garden enjoying his creation. *A Tea for All Seasons* can be used to enhance any of these times.

Tea is "an occasion of warmth and sociability between two or more people," says M. Dalton King. With *A Tea for All Seasons* as your foundation,

Just the simple act of putting on the kettle and waiting for the water to boil is an act of slowing down, of pausing, of anticipation.

teatime can be warm and sociable in many ways. You can have a special devotional time just you and the Lord, or you can invite friends, family or neighbors to join the two of you.

Often, our time with the Lord can become routine. But it could be a special, celebrated time. After all, we have an invitation to be with the King of Kings! *A Tea for All Seasons* is your invitation to tea with him.

Food for Thought

You'll notice that each devotion is accompanied by a recipe. I call the combination of a recipe with an accompanying Scripture passage "Food for Thought." But there is more to the "Food for Thought" method than simply having a cup of tea and a cookie with your daily devotions. Just like the phrase, this way of commemorating a spiritual principle with food has been around for a very long time. Traditional celebrations such as Passover and Communion were established by God to remind his people what he had done for them.

Each recipe selected corresponds in some way to the Scripture passage the devotion is based on. The pairing of the two serves different purposes.

First, the more we interact with anything we are learning, the more likely we are to remember it. The act of preparing the food can become part of the learning process as we allow the time spent to help embed the idea from the Scripture passage. Terry Willits, author of *Creating a SenseSational Home* says, "The more senses involved in any experience, the more we will retain its memory." Reading words on a page only stimulates us in a couple of ways, but the feel of the ingredients, the sound of the spoon scraping the bowl, the smell of fresh baked goodies, will all enhance the thoughts expressed in each devotion and make it a more complete experience.

As you begin to incorporate this new way of learning, you'll find there is another advantage. With each devotion there's more than enough to share. Opening your home to share teatime treats will open your heart to share special thoughts from Scripture.

Make your teatime a time with the Lord unlike any other.

There are as many ways to use this book as there are women who will read it. *A Tea for All Seasons* is about learning to see God in the different seasons of our lives. Make your teatime a time with the Lord unlike any other. I like to imagine a chair reserved for him. Although he may not physically partake of the tea and treats with me, his presence there can be very real.

A Tea for All Seasons can be the foundation for a number of different experiences.

You can enjoy a special time with the Lord yourself and then share what you discovered from Scripture as you share the treat with family and friends. Or you can plan ahead and invite someone else to be a part of your special moments of refreshment. Maybe you've never had a traditional devotional time and would like to begin with something fun.

Perhaps you do have a regular "quiet time," but you're looking for a new way to have a special time of celebration with the Lord.

You might be a Bible study group leader looking for new material and a new format for your group.

Or maybe you already "do" tea, and you'd like a fresh way to share God's Word with your guests.

The common thread is a desire for special time with the Lord. You can make most of these recipes ahead and then save the treat until you have the devotion, or make the whole process a part of your special quiet time. If you plan to use this method for a group, it's a good idea to make the food and do the devotion yourself, then share what you discovered with the group.

> *The simple act of writing something down embeds it into your heart and mind.*
>
>

I also like to keep a notebook or journal nearby. It's helpful to record what God says through the passage of Scripture or illustration. This helps especially when you want to share what you've discovered with others. Even if you don't intend to read it aloud, the simple act of writing something down embeds it into your heart and mind. It also gives something concrete to return to as you remember where you've been and what God has taught you.

Although you may never have used a format like this, with just a little planning and an excitement to meet the Lord, you may find new ways of your own to bring times of refreshment into your life.

The Basic Ingredients for a Beautiful Tea Time

Tea is grown primarily in mountain foothills of Asia, although South America and Africa also produce tea. The combination of tropical temperatures and rain, sunshine and shade are necessary for the growth spurts that produce the tender new leaves that are harvested for tea.

Green tea is processed the least and produces a fairly strong, often slightly bitter, tea. Just after the leaves are picked, green tea is "steamed" immediately to stop any oxidization or "fermentation." Fermentation results in darkening of the leaves and a mellowing of the taste of the tea.

After steaming, the leaves are rolled. This breaks the membranes in the leaves allowing the flavor to be released more readily. The rolled leaves are then heated to complete the drying process.

Black teas are "withered" after picking. The leaves are placed in a cool room and moisture is allowed to evaporate from the leaves and the fermentation process begins. Rolling takes place after withering, and then the leaves are left to continue to ferment for up to a day. Next, the leaves are fired to remove all but three percent of the original moisture. Black tea has the mellowest flavor, although it can be very intense.

Oolong teas are processed in a manner between green and black tea. The leaves are allowed to ferment briefly after picking. Once the leaves have reached their characteristically fruity scent, they are fired to prevent any further fermentation.

Choosing and Brewing Tea

You may have noticed the growing selection of teas in the supermarket, but you still reach for the familiar red and yellow box of basic tea bags. With just a little more information, you can be sure that every time you purchase a new tea you are getting exactly what you want.

First, you need to decide where to buy tea. Although there are more and more choices available at the supermarket, you will probably find that there are many other places in your community that offer even more variety.

> *Whether you are in the tea aisle at the market or in a specialty tea shop, there are some basics to know.*

For example, because of the growing popularity of tea, many places known for roasting and selling good quality coffee will also have very nice tea selections.

Whether you are in the tea aisle at the market or in a specialty tea shop, there are some basics to know about what you are looking for.

The first consideration is whether you'll buy loose tea or tea bags. Loose teas require either an infuser to contain the tea leaves while they are brewing, or a strainer to prevent the leaves from pouring into the teacup after the tea is brewed. Although tea bags are neater because they are self-contained, the tea that is in them is often of lower quality than that sold as loose tea.

Loose tea is generally whole leaf tea, while tea bags are often made of either a lower grade tea leaf or the particles left over from processing whole leaf tea. Although there are some companies now devoted to using the best quality leaves even in their tea bags, the best tea is still used in loose teas.

Once you've decided what type of tea to use, you need to decide whether you are looking for true tea or herbal "tea"; flavored or not; black, green, or oolong tea; and whether you are looking for Chinese, Indian, African or some other tea.

The location of the tea plantation does affect the flavor of the tea, just as wine grapes grown in Napa, California produce different wines than grapes grown in Bordeau, France. Although it is a matter of personal preference, it is good to learn whether you prefer the Ceylon tea grown in Sri Lanka, the Darjeeling tea grown in India, or Formosa tea from China. Many brands of tea are actually blends that a company develops to exploit the best traits of various teas. If the tea is a blend, it will often be referred to simply as black tea. If it is tea exclusively from one region, the label will usually specify that.

Tea selections also vary according to flavorings added to the tea. Teas are often flavored or "scented" with essential oils, dried fruits, flowers, herbs, or spices. Most packaged teas list the additional flavorings so you will have an idea of the flavor even before you purchase the tea.

Generally, the darker the tea, the greater the caffeine content. Therefore, green tea has less caffeine than oolong tea, and oolong less caffeine than black tea. Even black tea though, has less than half the caffeine content of coffee.

If the label says "Herbal Tea" it means the contents are a blend of herbs, spices, flowers and other flavorings and contain no actual tea leaves. Because there is no tea in it, there is also no caffeine content.

With each recipe that accompanies the devotion I've suggested a particular tea that I think complements that food. Certainly, you can drink any tea you enjoy with these treats, but if you'd like to try some new teas, you can use my suggestions as a guide.

In general, if I refer to a flavored tea such as raspberry or almond, you'll find that these are most often flavored black teas. If you are concerned about caffeine content, many black teas (even the flavored ones) are available de-caffeinated just like coffee.

Once you've decided on the tea, there are a couple of other things that are important to know to have the most enjoyable cup of tea.

Fresh, pure water is important for getting the best flavor from whichever tea you choose. If your local water doesn't have the cleanest taste, it might be worth it to use bottled drinking water. It doesn't have to be fancy designer water—just water with no other flavors of its own. Even though boiling water will kill impurities, it doesn't remove unpleasant tastes.

Many people are mysti-fied by the process of mak-ing a good pot of tea, but it isn't difficult once you know the basics. First, put fresh cool water into a tea kettle. If there is any water remain-ing from the last boiling, remove it. Boiling removes

Once you've decided on the tea, there are a couple of other things that are important to know to have the most enjoyable cup of tea.

oxygen from the water, and if you boil it too long or reuse it, your tea will taste flat. For green and oolong teas it is best to allow the water to come just to a boil. Black and herbal teas release their flavors better when the water has come to a full rolling boil.

While the water is boiling, run hot water from the tap into your serv-ing tea pot to allow it to warm. This keeps the water as hot as possible so you get maximum flavor from the tea.

The tea itself can be placed in the bottom of the warmed teapot and strained into the teacup after brewing; or it can be placed in a tea strainer and removed from the pot when the tea has reached its desired strength. Tea bags can be used in a pinch or when you can't find a particular flavor as loose tea. Herbal teas are often only available in bags.

Depending on your preferences, tea can be flavored with lemon or sweetened with honey or sugar. In England, milk is often added to black tea, especially when served to children.

Tea is more than a beverage

A special teatime is more than a great cup of tea. Around the world there are lots of sweets and goodies made to accompany the soothing brew. I've selected recipes from countries around the globe to accompany our special teatimes. Although you may never have tried many of these treats, don't let an unusual ingredient here or there intimidate you. Most of these ingredients are available in supermarkets everywhere and are not costly. Occasionally I've suggested a suitable substitution for a hard-to-find or expensive ingredient. And while some of the shapes may seem complicated, most of these recipes are very easy.

I've discovered some tricks that may simplify the baking process for you as well. For just a few dollars, it is worth the investment to purchase a roll of baking parchment to line your baking sheets. The parchment prevents cookies from sticking to the sheets. This is especially helpful for fragile cookies or those with fillings that may be especially sticky. In addition, the parchment eliminates the need to grease or butter the sheets, cutting down on the amount of added fat. The baking sheets also stay clean.

A special teatime is more than a great cup of tea.

When making rolled cookies, I found that using a pastry cloth and rolling pin cover makes the dough roll easier and you don't need to use as much flour to keep it from sticking. These are usually available together in kitchen shops and supermarkets.

Although I sometimes used cutters with fancy shapes or edges for the food in the photographs, you really don't need special equipment for these recipes. Most have been around for a long time so they can be made using the simplest of kitchen tools. The rim of a glass works for cutting out circles of dough, a plain muffin tin produces little cakes that taste as good as those baked in fancy molds, and a sharp knife can be used rather than a pastry wheel when making *Love Letters* or *Apricots en Chemise*.

So, if you're willing to try new things, you should find several recipes that will become new family favorites, and learn a little more about what we share in common with our neighbors around the world.

A World of Tea

In the Western world we often think of tea as primarily British—tea and crumpets or scones. We often forget that not only was tea consumed in Asia for centuries before it was imported to Europe, but an entire religious ceremony was created around tea. Just as tea traditions around the world vary from social to religious to nutritious, so do the types and manner of tea consumption.

Just as tea traditions around the world vary from social to religious to nutritious, so do the types and manner of tea consumption.

It is said that a Chinese Emperor, Shen Nung, discovered tea while out exploring his territory. Having learned that people who drank boiled water lived longer, he had his servants boiling water over a fire of camellia branches. Some of the leaves dropped into the water and the emperor found the brew delicious. He was certain it must be medicinal as well and began to promote its consumption.

The Chinese grow much of the tea produced today in the southeastern portion of their continent. Although they grow many varieties of tea, the Chinese drink more green and oolong tea than black tea.

The religious tea ceremony that originated in China is now more important and commonplace in Japan. Initially, tea was imported to Japan, however today it is actively cultivated there.

Japanese drink almost exclusively green tea. "Matcha" is a powdered green tea that is whipped to a froth with a bamboo whisk. It is the only type of tea used in the formal Japanese tea ceremony.

The Dutch were the first to import tea from Asia to Europe. It was shipped along with other valuable cargo of spices and rich fabrics. Before long the Dutch were trading with France and Britain as well.

The French probably enjoy the greatest variety of teas today. Carole Manchester said that "[in France] there is a tea for every mood, a tea for every hour of the day." Salons de Thé are as famous for their tea as the patisseries are for pastry. There is a growing trend in France that incorporates tearooms into bookshops—one of my favorite ideas. Teashops sell a variety of teas from around the world, often with as many as four hundred types and flavors including special house blends. Some teashops will even custom blend teas for their customers.

Russians adopted the French manner of tea in the late nineteenth century. The centerpiece of Russian teatime is the "samovar," a brass or silver urn used to brew and serve the tea. No matter what their income level, Russians are famous for their hospitality and teatime offers an opportunity to share their delicious breads and pastries. Russian tea is usually strong and often bitter, but it is served with a spoonful of cherry preserves placed in the bottom of the glass cup that sits in a metal holder. The custom is to drink the tea through a cube of sugar held between the teeth.

We are most familiar with the British traditions of tea, although many people are unaware that they have three different teatime traditions. A "Cream Tea" is usually a simple snack of tea and a scone with jam and "clotted" cream. "Afternoon Tea" is the wonderful traditional tea that begins with small, delicate sandwiches, then brings scones with jam and cream and concludes with a number of assorted cakes and pastries.

"High Tea" is often used incorrectly to describe Afternoon Tea. A true High Tea is a more substantial, less fancy meal. It was usually a working class meal taken in place of supper. High tea is often a meal that uses whatever is in the house: leftover meat and potatoes, always bread and usually cheese. Of course tea flows throughout the meal which is often finished off with cake.

India is the largest producer of tea in the world today. Their tea is often as spicy as the food that it accompanies, flavored with many of the spices for which India is famous. Although "chai" is simply the Indian word for tea, it has now come to mean a delicious, spicy concoction of black tea with spices such as ginger, cinnamon, cloves, cardamom and pepper. Chai is brewed with milk and sweetened with vanilla and honey. This brew is gaining popularity in American cafés, often as a transitional drink for those seeking to switch from coffee to tea. Although the tea flavor is hidden among all the spices, it is one of my favorite beverages. The cheerful spiciness is a great mood-lifter (and a nice balance to a rich chocolate fudge cake).

In Australia, tea is enjoyed as much in the outback as in cafés in the cities. Tea is brewed in the wilds in a tin cup called a "billy" over an open fire. Water is boiled in the billy and the tea leaves are placed in a wire mesh ball and dipped into the water. The tea is usually sweetened with sugar, although some-times a gum leaf is added for flavor.

As tea ties me to people all over the world, I enjoy knowing that my relation-ship with Jesus Christ ties me to people all the over the world as well.

Although we don't often think of Africans as tea drinkers, Kenya is actually one of the fastest growing exporters of tea. African tea is generally of the black variety. The foods served are of British influence, but pineapple fritters and "fru fru's," a sweet made with baked mashed yams, are indigenous treats. Teatime in Africa is a social occasion for neighbors to gather together from distant farms.

North Africa's Morocco has its own teatime traditions. Moroccan tea has a green tea base, but almost equal parts of mint are added. It is served sweetened with sugar—almost syrupy. The tea is commonly available on the streets of Morocco from vendors who carry portable tea urns on their backs.

Tea was an important commodity in early America, although the most famous tea party of all (the Boston Tea Party) precipitated a tea boycott here. Americans are second only to the British in tea consumption, although any sort of traditional teatime is newly back in vogue. Iced tea is America's one unique contribution to the world of tea.

As tea ties me to people all over the world, I enjoy knowing that my relationship with Jesus Christ ties me to people all over the world as well. Even though they both can be enjoyed alone, there is something special about knowing that somewhere, someone else is sipping a cup of tea, enjoy-ing a treat and savoring a special moment with the Lord. I hope you'll enjoy this unique teatime tradition.

A Time for Everything

God has made everything beautiful in its time.
Ecclesiastes 3:11

Melting Moments

This cookie, of Scottish origin, lives up to its name. Make these as a reminder that while time may be short, it can be very sweet if we learn to appreciate the beauty of each moment.

1/3 cup butter

1/3 cup sugar

1/8 teaspoon vanilla extract

1 egg

1 1/4 cups self rising flour

about 1/3 cup quick-cooking rolled oats or lightly crushed corn flakes

Preheat oven to 375 degrees.

In medium bowl, cream together butter and sugar until light and fluffy. Add vanilla extract and egg and beat well. Fold in flour until well mixed.

Make batter into 1-inch balls (about 1/2 tablespoon of batter) and roll in quick-cooking oats or corn flakes.

Place balls on greased baking sheet and bake for about 10 minutes or until tops are light golden and bottoms are very lightly browned. Cool briefly on baking sheet then remove to wire rack to cool completely. Makes about 2 dozen (recipe can be doubled). Melting Moments *are nice with a ginger or almond-flavored tea.* 🌿

A Time for Everything

There is a time for everything,
   and a season for every activity under heaven:

   a time to be born and a time to die,
   a time to plant and a time to uproot,
   a time to kill and a time to heal,
   a time to tear down and a time to build,
   a time to weep and a time to laugh,
   a time to mourn and a time to dance,
   a time to scatter stones and a time to gather them,
   a time to embrace and a time to refrain,
   a time to search and a time to give up,
   a time to keep and a time to throw away,
   a time to tear and a time to mend,
   a time to be silent and a time to speak,
   a time to love and a time to hate,
   a time for war and a time for peace.

—Ecclesiastes 3:1–8

Look around the room where you sit. Do you see a calendar? A clock? Are you wearing a wristwatch?

We have created all manner of items to *keep* time, but all they really do is keep *track* of time. It's difficult to grasp a definition of time. And perhaps even more difficult to grab on to time itself. Just as a drop of water is swept away indistinguishable from others in a stream, so do our moments slip away with time.

Time was one of God's first creations. In a previously dark world, God created light. Then he separated the light and the darkness and he called the light "day" and the dark "night" and there was morning and there was evening—the first day. After that, morning and evening were used to mark the work that God did.

I've heard preachers say that to God there is no passing of time as we define it by hours and minutes. A.W. Tozer said, "How completely satisfying to turn from our own limitations to a God who has none. Eternal years lie in his heart. For him, time does not pass, it remains . . ." In the scope of eternity, there is no *passage* of time. There is always as much time to come as there is time that has already been.

Certainly, events occur in what we perceive as a linear manner, but when Scripture says that Jesus Christ is the "same yesterday, today and forever" maybe a part of that means that with God, there is only NOW. Events may come and go, but the only moment is this one.

Think of what that means if we can begin to see time in God's terms rather than ours! Maybe time wholly devoted to God becomes "God's Time." That is, time on God's terms. When we commune with Him, perhaps we "turn from our limitations" and move beyond the scope of our sixty-minute hour and twenty-four-hour day. It is exciting to consider, don't you think?

I think George Muller would agree. As founder of a number of orphanages during the 1800's, there were many days when George found himself with more tasks than time in a given day. On those days, rather than cut his time with the Lord short, he spent extra time on his knees praying for strength and provision. He never regretted his choice.

We can't gather up moments and store them for later use. We can't anticipate the time to come and catch it before it slips away. Once we realize that time can't be banked or hoarded, we see that the best we can do is make the most of what time we do have.

It's not about working harder or laughing more, but an awareness and appreciation of the uniqueness of the time we have. Although it is often said that there is no time like the present, the truth is that there is no time *but* the present. So I hope you will enjoy the moments contained and reflected upon within these pages, and that at the end you'll see that time spent listening for the Lord's voice is a wise investment.

A Season for Every Activity

. . . for signs and for seasons and for days and for years . . .
Genesis 1:14 (NASB)

Half Moon Cookies

This cookie, which looks like the quarter moon, can illustrate that just as the seasons in nature are perpetual and each serves a purpose, so the seasons in our lives will never stand still and each plays a part in the creation of our character.

1 1/4 cups flour
1/2 cup powdered sugar
1/4 teaspoon baking powder
1/2 teaspoon ground cardamom
    or allspice
1/8 teaspoon salt
1/2 cup (1 stick) chilled butter,
    cut in pieces

1 egg yolk
1 teaspoon vanilla
about 1/2 cup fruit preserves
    (not jam or jelly)
1 egg white beaten with
    2 teaspoons milk
decorating sugar or raw sugar

In medium bowl, sift together flour, powdered sugar, baking powder, cardamom and salt. Cut in butter with pastry blender or two knives; texture should be like coarse crumbs.

In another bowl, beat vanilla with egg yolk. Add to flour mixture and stir until moistened. Form dough into a ball, cover with plastic wrap and refrigerate for an hour or longer. (Dough can be made in advance and refrigerated for several days to be baked fresh when needed.)

When ready to bake, preheat oven to 350 degrees. Remove dough from refrigerator. Grease baking sheets or line with parchment.

Divide dough into two or three pieces and pat into circles. Flour rolling pin and work surface. Roll dough to 1/8-inch thickness. Using a round cutter, cut dough into 3-inch circles.

Brush a little water or milk around edges of dough; place 1/4 teaspoon of preserves in center of circle. Fold in half and press edges together gently. Be sure the edges are well sealed, and seal any cracks in dough so preserves won't melt out while baking.

continued on next page ...

Brush lightly with glaze and sprinkle with decorating sugar. Place filled half moons on prepared baking sheets, 1 inch apart. Bake for 10–12 minutes or until golden brown on bottoms and light golden on tops.

Cool on wire racks and store in airtight containers. Cookies will keep 2 to 3 days at room temperature or can be frozen for longer storage. *Serve Half Moon Cookies with a tea that complements the flavor of the filling you use.* 🍂

> *The moon marks off the seasons,*
>   *and the sun knows when to go down.*
>   —Psalm 104:19

"Day and night do not share the sky. They take turns with it ... One precludes the other, but both are needed to complete the natural order," said Dr. E.C. Krupp. The sun and moon, offering light and heat, and time and tide, work together to create the seasons of the earth.

The very earliest farmers depended on the moon in helping them know when it would be safe to plant without danger of killing frost and when to harvest the crops for maximum yield. Gardeners still follow much of the same lore regarding planting, pruning and harvesting during various phases of the moon.

Sara Stein has observed the cycles set in motion by the sun and the moon and recorded them in her book *Noah's Garden*. She notes that the birds arrive from their wintering grounds just as the insects upon which they feed are hatching. The protein the insects provide is necessary for the birds' breeding season. Grapes don't ripen until the birds need fuel for their fall migrations, even though the grapes have no awareness of the birds' feeding patterns.

The earth and its inhabitants cannot exist in one endless season. Even the most extreme continent, the Antarctic, has seasonal cycles that are required to sustain the life that dwells there.

What is your favorite time of year? Although some say that California has an almost endless summer, I like the fall season here. It isn't as spectacular as other regions—there's no abundance of brilliant foliage or crisp, cold days that signal the change. The transition here is more subtle: the bright summer sunshine gives way to a deeper golden glow that casts a rich light over everything; the soft summer breeze picks up a cool edge that rattles across the pavement with the fallen leaves.

Evelyn H. Lauder said, "We do not have to choose our favorites among the seasons. It is only necessary to rejoice in the beauty of their differences." But far beyond the seasonal changes of nature, we need to see the beauty of the seasonal changes in our lives. Just as freezing temperatures are necessary for the maple tree to release the sweetness that forms deep inside, sometimes it is necessary to endure extremes in our lives to find the wealth we have inside. Chuck Swindoll said, "Seasons are designed to deepen us, to instruct us in the wisdom and ways of our God."

We sometimes have difficulty seeing the value in various seasons in our lives. We rejoice in the warmth of happy times but avoid the frost of loneliness; we try to avoid the toil of seedtime yet anxiously await the abundant harvest that comes only at the end of a productive season.

Each of us will face a variety of seasons in our lifetime. In some cases the seasons are bold and distinctive. At other times the changes are subtle. But just as God has a plan for the time that plants bloom and insects hatch, he has a plan for the occurrences in our lives as well.

And as we acknowledge the Master Plan the Creator set in motion, we can take confidence in knowing that our lives are not left to chance or random happenstance. We have the assurance that all things will come together to produce maturity and, ultimately, to bring glory to the Creator.

Throughout the following pages we'll take a look at some of the activities that may occur as you and I walk through the seasons of our lives. I hope that our time will bring us a new appreciation of the seasons the Creator has planned for each of us.

After all, God has promised:

As long as the earth endures, seedtime and harvest, cold and heat, summer and winter, day and night will never cease.

—Genesis 8:22

A Time to Plant

Sow your seed in the morning.
Ecclesiastes 11:6

Seedcake

This recipe is filled with flavorful seeds in a rich cake. Serve it as a reminder that we should be willing to drop the seeds of God's Word wherever there is an opportunity. He'll take care of the rest.

1/2 cup (1 stick) butter, softened

3/4 cup sugar

1 tablespoon caraway seeds

1 teaspoon ground cardamom

2 1/2 cups flour

1 teaspoon baking powder

pinch salt

1/4 cup milk

3 eggs

Powdered sugar

Preheat oven to 350 degrees. Grease 8-inch round by 3-inch deep cake pan. (A small springform pan will work well.)

In large bowl, cream together butter and sugar until light and fluffy. Stir in caraway seeds and cardamom.

Sift together flour, baking powder and salt. In a small bowl, beat milk and eggs together. Add dry ingredients to butter mixture a little at a time, alternating with milk mixture. Beat well after each addition.

Pour into well-greased cake pan and bake 45 minutes, or until toothpick inserted in center comes out clean. Cool for 5 minutes in pan, then turn onto wire rack and cool completely. Sprinkle powdered sugar onto cake before serving. Seedcake *is good with the slightly citrus taste of Earl Grey tea.*

A Time to Plant

"Then He told them many things in parables, saying: 'A farmer went out to sow his seed. As he was scattering the seed, some fell along the path, and the birds ate it up. Some fell on rocky places, where it did not have much soil. It sprang up quickly, because the soil was shallow. But when the sun came up, the plants were scorched, and they withered because they had no root. Other seed fell among thorns, which grew up and choked the plants. Still other seed fell on good soil where it produced a crop . . . But the one who received the seed that fell on good ground is the man who hears the word and understands it. He produces a crop, yielding a hundred, sixty, or thirty times what was sown."
—Matthew 13:3–8, 23

I have to admit that I don't have much of a green thumb. It doesn't stop me from trying, however. I just know that my results might not be as showy as someone else's. When I was young, my parents gave my sister and me a row in the garden to plant whatever we wanted. I don't remember much about that garden except that it produced watermelons so small I could take a whole one to school in my lunch!

I've taken classes about gardening, observed what my feeble attempts have produced, and admired the results that others are able to cultivate. I've realized that I can't predict when a crop will be fruitful or not. There are so many variables that determine what the yield of fruits or flowers will actually be.

Outside of a greenhouse or laboratory, there is no way to control all the variables or to anticipate the precise outcome of our efforts.

Usually, we think of planting in a garden—someplace where we have some influence and control. We can work the soil so that it is not too hard or rocky for the seed to have protection. We can add things to the soil that will help it retain water, yet drain well so the seed won't rot. We can control the amount of water so that even in the harshest sunlight, the plants won't wither.

Things that grow in the wild are a whole different matter, though. All we can do is watch to see what takes root and how it grows. We can't determine whether there will be enough rain for the grasses and flowers to be productive. We don't know whether the rest of the plant and animal world will do their part to spread the seeds and pollinate the flowers so the production can continue.

Even though we don't generally think of planting anything in the wild, American history tells us of John Chapman, who became known as Johnny Appleseed. He left his home and moved westward, planting apple orchards along the way. He didn't always know whether an orchard would really be fruitful or not. He just planted the seeds and trusted that God would do the rest.

I think sharing the news of the kingdom of God can be like that. Sharing the word of God within our families, especially with children, can be like planting in a garden. We can make sure the rocks and weeds have been removed, supply plenty of refreshing water and protect them from influences that will snatch the seed away.

Because we don't usually think of planting seeds in the wild where we can't control the conditions, we also don't often scatter the seeds of God's word in the uncertain terrain of an unknown heart. Often we make judgments about the condition of the heart we're trying to reach and assume that there are already too many weeds or rocks to bother planting the seed there at all. Sometimes we see the scars caused by flames of sin and assume that nothing could possibly grow there.

At a college Bible study, a visiting speaker told the students about a woman from his church who received a prank phone call in the middle of the night. Rather than hanging up on the caller, she stayed on the line. When she had an opportunity to speak, she told him how Jesus had died to take his place for his wrongdoings, and that he could be forgiven and begin a new life in Christ. The woman didn't know what impact her words had, but she knew she had planted the seed.

After the meeting, one of the students from the group approached the speaker and told him that several years ago his brother had lived in the area the woman was from and made a prank call to a woman who shared the Gospel message with him. The student's brother is now in ministry himself and says that the gospel message he heard over the phone led to a permanent change in his life.

Although we don't know for certain that the brother is the same young man that the woman shared with, it certainly illustrates that no matter how obscure or impossible the opportunity, God really can work wonders when we are faithful to do our part.

Maybe, when it comes to sharing the message of God, we should be like the woman on the phone—and Johnny Appleseed—planting the seeds and trusting God to do the rest to help them take root and be fruitful.

A Time to Heal

Your Father knows what you need before you ask him.
Matthew 6:18

Beggar's Purse

The Beggar's Purse, *with its sweet surprise hidden inside, can show us that God always gives us what we* need, *even when we only ask Him for what we want.*

1 pound phyllo sheets
1/2 cup (1 stick) unsalted butter or margarine, melted
2 cups finely chopped, tart apples (about 3 medium-sized apples)
1/2 cup golden raisins or other chopped, dried fruit
2 tablespoons honey

Preheat oven to 350 degrees. Peel and chop apples. Add raisins or other fruit and honey. Mix until fruit is coated with honey. Set aside.

Place 1 phyllo sheet on work surface, brush with melted butter*, covering entire surface lightly. Place another sheet on top, brushing with butter. Repeat until there are 4 buttered sheets stacked on top of each other.

Cut stack into 4-inch squares. Using slotted spoon, place 1 teaspoon of filling into center of square (do not put any extra juice in with filling—it will leak out and make the bottoms soggy). Be careful not to overfill or phyllo will split. Gently bring corners together over filling and crimp slightly to create "purse." Place on parchment lined baking sheet, 1 inch apart. Bake one cooking sheet at a time for 20 minutes or until deep golden and crisp. Allow to cool on baking sheet and serve. Makes about 3 dozen. *Very good with cinnamon or other spice-flavored tea.*

* *Butter-flavored cooking spray can be used on each layer of phyllo in place of melted butter.*

A Time to Heal

As Jesus approached Jericho, a blind man was sitting by the roadside begging. When he heard the crowd going by, he asked what was happening. They told him, "Jesus of Nazareth is passing by."

He called out, "Jesus, Son of David, have mercy on me!"

Those who led the way rebuked him and told him to be quiet, but he shouted all the more, "Son of David have mercy on me!"

Jesus stopped and ordered the man to be brought to him. When he came near, Jesus asked him, "What do you want me to do for you?"

"Lord I want to see," he replied.

Jesus said to him, "Receive your sight; your faith has healed you." Immediately he received his sight and followed Jesus, praising God. When all the people saw it, they also praised God.

—Luke 18:35–43

My parents have been involved in Rescue Mission work since I was a child, and our town is a popular destination for homeless people. As a result, I've been around beggars most of my life. I've seen that usually when beggars are asked what they want, they will ask to have their most immediate need met. They will ask for money, maybe food, sometimes shelter; although not as often as you might expect. I have never heard a beggar ask for long-term employment or medical care to heal an ailment that prevents him from making his way in the world.

That's why I am surprised at the blind beggar's request to be made able to see. Unlike others that Jesus healed, this man was "working" at the time, not seeking healing. Unlike most of the others Jesus healed, this man seemed to be more concerned with meeting his immediate needs than eliminating his primary problem.

That is, until Jesus asked the man, "What do you want me to do for you?" The man showed his understanding of who Jesus was by asking to be able to see. If the blind man had perceived Jesus to be a great leader or simply the "celebrity" of the moment, he might have asked for money or food or to be taken care of. However, he knew Jesus could heal his deepest weakness.

Unfortunately, when we approach God, we often are seeking a quick solution to our immediate discomfort, rather than complete healing of our deepest deficiency.

Joan Wester Anderson tells the story of Mark, who was scheduled for back surgery. He went to a pastor to pray for healing, but the surgery took place as planned, followed by a long convalescence. Two years later, Mark returned to thank the minister for his prayer of healing.

The pastor was puzzled by Mark's attitude since he wasn't freed from the need for surgery and didn't experience a rapid recovery.

Mark explained that at the time of his surgery his family was in turmoil; his wife had filed for divorce, he was estranged from one child and a second was on drugs. During the time of his recovery though, the family came together to care for Mark. In the process they were able to resolve many of their problems and restore the family. The pain of the surgery and the recuperation were temporary, but the restoration of the family was permanent.

Mark told the pastor he was grateful for the healing of his family. God knew that the physical problem was not the most important ailment in Mark's life. Mark said, "God provided the healing I needed rather than the one I thought I wanted."

Have you ever found, like me, that when you approach God for a "healing," you don't actually bring your deepest needs to him? Like many beggars, we ask God to take away the hunger, without recognizing that we really need to regain our sight so that we can work and earn our own way. Instead, we often ask for what we think we need immediately. If we are having financial troubles, we'll ask for money and look for checks in the mail, when the answer may be to find a way to earn some extra money. If a relationship is causing problems, sometimes we'll ask for the problem behaviors to change rather than asking God to work in the hearts that need to be made right with Him and look for opportunities to help improve the situation ourselves.

We can be thankful though, that God is not limited by our requests. It's so encouraging to know that God will always meet our needs, even when we ask for only what we think we want.

And my God will meet all your needs according to his glorious riches in Christ Jesus.

Philippians 4:19

A Time to Tear Down

First take the plank out of your own eye, and then you will see clearly to remove the speck from your brother's eye.

Matthew 7:5

Date Planks

These rich log cookies can be a reminder that it is more important for us to deal with our own flaws and shortcomings before we worry about others.

1 1/2 cups flour

1 teaspoon baking powder

1 teaspoon salt

3 eggs

1 1/2 cups light brown sugar (packed)

1 1/2 cups (8 oz) pitted, chopped dates

3/4 cup chopped walnuts or pecans

Preheat oven to 350 degrees. In medium bowl, mix together flour, baking powder and salt. Add dates and toss gently to coat with flour mixture. Set aside.

In large bowl, beat eggs until light and frothy. Beat in the brown sugar. Gradually mix in flour and dates. Fold in nuts.

Spread mixture into a greased 9 x 13-inch baking pan. Bake for 30 minutes or until top is light brown and toothpick inserted into center comes out clean.

Cool in pan for about 15 minutes, then cut into 1/2-inch by 3-inch "planks." Cool on wire rack and store in airtight container. *Serve* Date Planks *with any rich, flavorful tea.*

A Time to Tear Down

"Do not judge, or you too will be judged. For in the same way you judge others, you will be judged, and with the measure you use, it will be measured to you.

Why do you look at the speck of sawdust in your brother's eye and pay no attention to the plank in your own eye? How can you say to your brother, 'Let me take the speck out of your eye,' when all the time there is a plank in your own eye? You hypocrite, first take the plank out of your own eye, and then you will see clearly to remove the speck from your brother's eye.'"

—Matthew 7:1–5

While working in the yard one day, my mom turned at just the wrong moment and got poked in the eye with a peach branch. It took a doctor over an hour to remove all the debris, and she had to wear an eye patch for several days. Even after the patch was removed, the eye was bruised and sensitive for a long time, and she had to take care not to get other irritants in it. In a very real sense, she learned what most of us will never know about having a "log" in our eye.

Have you ever had to wear a patch, or for some other reason were unable to see clearly out of one eye? Do you remember how odd it was? The things that used to come easily now needed extra time and attention.

Try this—get a needle and thread, close one eye and try to thread the needle while holding it at least a foot from your eye. How long does it take you? Do you find yourself moving it closer to your open eye?

The problem is, when you have only one good eye, depth perception is lost, so you can't see very far or very accurately. Imagine trying to detect something small in another person's eye when you only have one eye to use. To make it more challenging there is a large object protruding out of your eye that makes it impossible to get close enough to really see what you are doing.

Often this passage is used to say that we are most likely to pick on a brother or sister for the same shortcomings we have in our own life—only ours are bigger. I think the same thing is true even when our shortcomings are very different from our neighbor's. There are areas that God wants to improve in our lives, but we are often so concerned with others' weaknesses that we look past our own.

There's an old carpenters' saying, "Measure twice, cut once." I think we can use that in our own lives when evaluating other people's shortcomings as well. We are quick to judge, to jump to conclusions, and we often can't wait to point out what we know. Oswald Chambers said, "Which of us would dare stand before God and say, 'My God, judge me as I have judged my fellow men' ? . . . The measure you mete out is measured to you again . . . If you have been shrewd in finding out the defects of others, that will be exactly the measure meted out to you; people will judge you in the same way."

When you and I look at the example we have—Jesus Christ—and take a good look at ourselves, we don't have time to worry about others' shortcomings. We have so far to go on our own that we could spend the rest of our lives trying to improve ourselves without being concerned about how others are doing. The habit of judging and condemning others can be a more serious blemish than the things we so glibly point out as others' faults.

Often, we use our critical abilities to see where we stand in relation to other people. When we believe that we are ahead of the game, at least in our own estimation, we use that as an excuse to back off on working on the areas where we fall short.

King David seemed to have the right idea. He had been appointed to succeed a corrupt king, a king who wanted to kill him. Yet even while he was running for his life, he recognized that he fell short of God's standards and often sought God to show him his shortcomings so that nothing would hinder his fellowship with God.

If we keep our eyes on the One we want to be most like, we will be less concerned with what those around us are doing.

Test me, O Lord, and try me, examine my heart and my mind.

Psalm 26:2

A Time to Build Up

The lips of the righteous nourish many.
Proverbs 22:11

Cats' Tongues (Langues-de-Chat)

It's hard to know whether this cookie is originally Italian, French or Spanish. Its name comes from its long, slender shape. Cats' Tongues *can help us remember to build one another up with our words, rather than being "catty."*

6 tablespoons unsalted butter, soft but not melted
1/2 cup superfine sugar
pinch of salt
1/2 teaspoon vanilla
2 egg whites
1/2 cup flour

Preheat oven to 400 degrees. Line several baking sheets with parchment or grease heavily with unsalted butter.

In small bowl, use electric mixer to beat together butter, sugar and salt until light and fluffy. Continue to beat on medium speed, adding vanilla and egg whites, then beating well after each addition.

Beat two more minutes, then gradually sift in flour, beating until batter is smooth.

Spoon mixture into pastry bag fitted with 1/4-inch tip, or plastic storage bag with very small portion of one corner cut off.

Pipe batter onto prepared baking sheets in 3-inch strips about the width of a pencil, 2 inches apart (cookies will spread a lot).

Bake 5 to 7 minutes or until golden at edges and pale in center. After cooling briefly, remove to wire racks to cool completely.

Store in airtight container or freeze well-wrapped cookies.

Allow baking sheets to cool completely and re-line or butter before baking next batch. Cats' Tongues *go especially well with a gently flavored orange tea.*

A Time to Build Up

From the fruit of his lips a man is filled with good things
  as surely as the work of his hands rewards him.

Truthful lips endure forever,
  but a lying tongue lasts only a moment.

A perverse man stirs up dissension,
  and a gossip separates close friends.

A wicked man listens to evil lips;
  a liar pays attention to a malicious tongue.

He who guards his mouth and his tongue
  keeps himself from calamity.

The lips of the righteous nourish many,
  but fools die for lack of judgment.

—Proverbs 12:14, 19; 16:28; 17:4; 21:23; 10:21

A fight consisting primarily of bitter words is called a "cat fight," and unkind remarks are "catty." You might understand where these terms come from if you've ever been licked by a cat. An exploring tongue that starts out feeling like wet velvet can become like irritating sandpaper.

Our tongues can be like that too, depending on the words we choose. We are capable of playful, ticklish, delightful gentleness as well as severe, scratchy, painful words that can leave the spirit of our "victims" raw and bleeding. Words of praise can build up and encourage. Angry or lying words can destroy a reputation or break a spirit.

Think about the people you most admire or most enjoy being around. When you describe them, are they described as "able to put someone in their place, sarcastic, having biting humor?" Or do you admire people who are described as "kind, gracious, never has a bad thing to say about anyone"?

Americans are known for their bluntness, for "telling it like it is." I would like to be known as gracious, but I'm afraid that too often when asked a direct question, I give a direct answer even if it is not necessarily kind or gracious. I do this even though I know that Colossians 4:6 says, "Let your speech be always full of grace, seasoned with salt, so that you may know how to answer everyone."

One person who has become an example of graciousness to me is Dr. Billy Graham. He recently appeared on "Larry King Live," a television show with a host who is known for being tough on guests. Larry King put Dr. Graham on the spot as he questioned him about his involvement with every president since the late '50s.

Dr. Graham said he learned a lesson about speaking out of turn after his first meeting with President Truman. The press asked Dr. Graham about his meeting the following day, and he answered their questions honestly. President Truman, however, made it very clear that the conversation was to have been just between the two of them. He never called on Billy Graham again, and Dr. Graham never made the same mistake.

In addition to not betraying what he discusses with heads of governments and other religious leaders, Dr. Graham has also developed a graciousness uncharacteristic of most Americans. When cornered about his opinions of other political and religious leaders, he always had something good to say, even though he did not necessarily count the men in question among his friends or agree with their politics. Larry King is not a great supporter of religious people or causes, yet his respect for Billy Graham was obvious.

The Bible has a great deal to say about the tongue. It addresses the dangers of talking too much, lying, gossiping and being unkind. God also tells how truthful, kind, restrained lips can nourish those who hear. My husband has a way of evaluating comments before he makes them. He asks, "Is it true? Is it kind? Is it necessary?"

Being gracious is not always easy. Sometimes there's a great temptation to take the quick opportunity to build ourselves up by belittling someone else. But our reputation will be protected and we will be honored if we can learn to speak kindly.

He who loves a pure heart and whose speech is gracious will have the king for a friend.

Psalm 10:21

A Time to Weep

For with much wisdom comes much sorrow.
Ecclesiastes 3:11

First Lady Cookies

Although they probably got their name for being a favorite around the White House, these crisp, sweet cookies can remind us of Eve and that sometimes knowledge can be a cause of sorrow. We'll have less cause for weeping in our own lives if we focus on things that are pure and true.

4 cups flour

1 teaspoon baking soda

1 cup (2 sticks) butter

2 cups sugar

3 eggs

Preheat oven to 350 degrees. Grease baking sheets or line with parchment.

Put flour into large mixing bowl, stir in baking soda. Melt butter in small saucepan. Pour hot butter steadily into flour, beating constantly. Beat in sugar, then beat in eggs.

On lightly floured surface, roll dough to 1/4-inch thickness. Cut in small rounds with cookie cutter and place 1 inch apart on baking sheets.

Bake for 12 to 15 minutes, until lightly golden. Cool on wire racks. Store in airtight container. *I like the buttery flavor of* First Lady Cookies *with a vanilla-flavored tea.*

A Time to Weep

Now the serpent was more crafty than any of the wild animals the Lord God had made. He said to the woman, "Did God really say, 'You must not eat from any tree in the garden?'"

The woman said to the serpent, "We may eat fruit from the trees in the garden, but God did say, 'You must not eat fruit from the tree that is in the middle of the garden, and you must not touch it or you will surely die.'"

"You will not surely die," the serpent said to the woman. "For God knows that when you eat of it your eyes will be opened, and you will be like God, knowing good and evil."

When the woman saw that the fruit of the tree was good for food and pleasing to the eye, and also desirable for gaining wisdom, she took some and ate it. She also gave some to her husband, who was with her and he ate it. Then the eyes of both of them were opened, and they realized that they were naked; so they sewed fig leaves together and made coverings for themselves.

—Genesis 3:1–7

The first lady of the world learned that too much knowledge can be a bad thing. What the serpent didn't tell Eve was that the knowledge she and Adam would gain by eating the fruit would bring sorrow and shame into their world.

Because the pursuit of knowledge has long been respected and admired, it's easy to overlook that there can be unhappy consequences from much learning. Maybe there is something to the old saying, "Ignorance is bliss."

King Solomon, known as the wisest man to ever live, put it this way, "Then I applied myself to the understanding of wisdom, and also of madness and folly, but I learned that this, too, is chasing after the wind. For with much wisdom comes much sorrow; the more knowledge, the more grief." (Ecclesiastes 1:17, 18).

We know this to be true for children. We take care to select books and videos that won't expose them to thoughts and ideas that can frighten them, harm them or lead them into bad choices. We don't always apply that same wisdom to our own choices, however. Movies, television shows, books and music can all expose us to thoughts and ideas that are anything but pure and uplifting.

We expose ourselves to unwholesome thoughts, visions or activities with the explanation that the knowledge will benefit us in some way. We justify questionable choices in music, books or movies by saying that we need to be aware of where our culture is going, ignoring the contaminating influence these things can have in our lives.

When Paul said that he became "all things to all men that by all possible means (he) might save some" (1 Corinthians 9:22), he did not mean that he participated in the acts of the pagans in order to be accepted by them. In his letter to the Corinthians, Paul tells them that they are to " . . . come out from them and be separate . . ." (2 Corinthians 6:17). We don't need to participate in the activities of the world in order to be heard by them.

Do you remember the song "Edelweiss" from the movie *The Sound of Music*? It tells of the Swiss national flower. Because edelweiss only grows on the highest peaks of the Alps, it must be sought out. It is prized for its unique beauty and purity. "Small and white, clean and bright," its whiteness is comparable only to the snow that serves as its backdrop. Even when picked and pressed in paper for preservation, it retains its pure color for years.

You and I should be like that, striving to reach the highest peaks in our journey with the Lord and maintaining our purity whatever our surroundings. Sometimes we give in to fear that we will not be able to impact the world if we live at the heights of holiness. If you look closely though, you'll see that the world has been striving to reach those peaks since the beginning of time. They just don't realize it isn't possible to do so without help. It is easier to help someone climb a mountain by giving them a hand up than it is to try to push them up from the valley floor. We can only be there to lead them up if we haven't allowed ourselves to be stuck in the mire of the world below.

"Finally brothers, whatever is true, whatever is noble, whatever is right, whatever is pure, whatever is lovely, whatever is admirable—if anything is excellent or praiseworthy—think about such things."

Philippians 4:8

A Time to Laugh

Blessed are you who weep now, for you will laugh.
Luke 6:21

White Wedding Cookies

Many countries have a version of this traditional cookie. They're a great reminder that just like it's worth the wait to find "the right one." God always provides just what we need at the right time.

1 cup butter, softened
1/2 cup confectioners' sugar
1 teaspoon vanilla extract
2 cups flour
1/4 teaspoon salt
1 teaspoon baking powder
3/4 cup toasted walnuts or pecans, finely chopped
confectioners' sugar

Preheat oven to 350 degrees. In large mixing bowl, cream together butter, powdered sugar and vanilla. Beat until light and fluffy.

Stir together flour, baking powder and salt. Gradually stir flour into butter mixture. Add pecans or walnuts, stirring until the nuts are evenly distributed.

If dough is too sticky to handle, refrigerate until firm. Break off 1-inch pieces of dough; roll into balls.

Place on ungreased baking sheets, 2 inches apart. Bake for 10 to 12 minutes or until set but still pale in color.

Cool slightly, then roll in confectioners' sugar. When cookies are completely cooled, roll in confectioners' sugar again.

Cookies can be frozen before they are coated with sugar. Allow to thaw completely, then coat with sugar and serve. White Wedding Cookies *are good with almond or any other nutty tea.* ❦

A Time to Laugh

On the third day a wedding took place at Cana in Galilee. Jesus' mother was there, and Jesus and his disciples had also been invited to the wedding. When the wine was gone, Jesus' mother said to him, "They have no more wine."

"Dear woman, why do you involve me?" Jesus replied, "My time has not yet come."

His mother said to the servants, "Do whatever he tells you."

Nearby stood six stone water jars, the type used by the Jews for ceremonial washing, each holding from twenty to thirty gallons.

Jesus said to the servants, "Fill the jars with water"; so they filled them to the brim. Then he told them, "Now draw some out and take it to the master of the banquet."

They did so, and the master of the banquet tasted the water that had been turned into wine. He did not realize where it had come from, though the servants who had drawn the water knew. Then he called the bridegroom aside and said, "Everyone brings out the choice wine first and then the cheaper wine after the guests have had too much to drink; but you have saved the best till now."

This, the first of his miraculous signs, Jesus performed at Cana in Galilee. He thus revealed his glory and his disciples put their faith in him.

—John 2:1–11

Are you a patient person? Are you content to wait for good things to come to you, or do you want them *now*?

In our impatient world, often we don't want to wait to have the best. College graduates want to come right out of school and walk into management level jobs that took their predecessors many years to achieve. Young couples just starting out want to purchase homes equivalent to the ones their parents owned after years of hard work. We see people eager to marry, forcing relationships that may not be the best simply because they're not content to wait for the Lord's provision for them.

Although it can be painful or frustrating, there can be good reasons to wait for God's best. Sometimes we need to mature in order to be good stewards of what He wants to give us. Maybe the waiting will allow us to be an encouragement to others who also struggle through the waiting process. Often, we appreciate whatever it is even more because we've been without before.

I spent several months as a church intern. The church arranged for me to live with a couple, Bob and Chris. After seventeen years of marriage and ten years of trying unsuccessfully to have a child, they dedicated themselves to working with the church high school group, enjoying their relationship and building their careers. Bob had a good job in the local city government and Chris was working on a Master's Degree in nursing.

Imagine their surprise when they found that Chris was pregnant! Although it was a risky pregnancy, Chris was willing to stay in bed and do what was necessary to ensure the birth of a healthy child.

When their healthy boy was born a couple of months after I left to return to college, I learned they named him Nathan, meaning "gift." The waiting made it even more apparent what a special blessing their son was.

Chris says that although the years of disappointment were difficult, she knows that God gave Nathan to them at just the right time—their gift was worth the wait.

In his book, *Parable of Joy*, Michael Card says of this passage that it's not so much about God saving the best for last as it is "saving the best for *now*." God doesn't wait for "later" just for the sake of waiting. He waits for the moment that will bring Him glory. Sometimes that moment means that a great number of people will understand the work He has done. Sometimes it means that we see His hand more clearly. But it always means that even though the wait may seem long, God's best for our lives and his perfect timing is worth the wait.

For the Lord is a God of justice. Blessed are all who wait for Him.

Isaiah 30:18

A Time to Scatter Stones

It is much more blessed to give than to receive.
Acts 20:35

Apricots en Chemise

"Chemise" is the French word for shirt. These cookies are "Apricots in a Shirt." They can help us remember that God will honor those who give extra even to their enemies.

12 fresh apricots	*glaze*
1 cup sugar	1/2 cup confectioners' sugar
1 pound puff pastry	1 tablespoon milk
2 eggs	
1/4 cup milk	

Preheat oven to 350 degrees. Peel apricots (peels remove easily if apricot is dropped briefly into boiling water). Cut apricots in half following "seam" from stem end. Remove pits. Sprinkle apricots with granulated sugar.

Roll puff pastry to 1/4-inch thickness. (If using frozen puff pastry, simply thaw and unroll sheets.) Using pastry wheel or sharp knife, cut into 3-inch squares. Place one apricot half in center of square. Using finger, spread a little milk around edges of square. Fold dough over apricot, pressing slightly to seal edges.

Mix eggs with milk; brush top of pastry with mixture. Place on parchment lined baking sheet.

Bake for 15 to 20 minutes, until pastry is puffy and golden. Transfer to wire rack to cool slightly. Mix milk and confectioners' sugar. Drizzle icing over pastry. Serve hot or cold.

These can be frozen prior to icing. Freeze in a single layer on baking sheet for about 1 hour. Place in airtight container with waxed paper between layers. To serve, defrost thoroughly, reheat in oven and drizzle with glaze. Apricots en Chemise *are wonderful with any black tea with apricot flavoring. Look for those that have apricot along with another flavor for an extra special taste.*

A Time to Scatter Stones

"But I tell you who hear me: Love your enemies, do good to those who hate you, bless those who curse you, pray for those who mistreat you. If someone strikes you on one cheek, turn to him the other also. If someone takes your cloak, do not stop him from taking your tunic. Give to everyone who asks you, and if anyone takes what belongs to you, do not demand it back. Do to others as you would have them do to you.

If you love those who love you, what credit is that to you? Even 'sinners' love those who love them. And if you do good to those who are good to you, what credit is that to you? Even 'sinners' do that. And if you lend to those from whom you expect repayment, what credit is that to you? Even 'sinners' lend to 'sinners,' expecting to be repaid in full. But love your enemies, do good to them and lend to them without expecting anything back. Then your reward will be great, and you will be the sons of the Most High, because he is kind to the ungrateful and wicked."

—Luke 6:27–35

If you've spent much time around young children, you've seen that one of the first words they learn to say is "mine." Ann Landers printed a piece called "The Toddler's Creed" that explains it like this:

If I want it, it's mine.
If it looks just like mine, it is mine.
If I can take it away from you it's mine.
If I give it to you and change my mind later, it's mine.
If we are building something together, all the pieces are mine.
If it's mine, it will never belong to anyone else, no matter what.

Sound familiar? These days, it's not just toddlers who act like that. "Mine" isn't a trait that we grow out of. Alarms, security systems, "The Club"—there are vast industries that exist simply to make sure that the things we possess stay ours.

Although my needs were met when I was growing up, I didn't have much of the abundance that I saw around me. Maybe that's why I've always found it difficult to be free with my own things. In fact, for most of my life, I would have believed that my middle name was "selfish," I heard it so often.

One gloomy afternoon when I was about 18 years old, I left our house and walked the four blocks to the downtown area, hoping to find someone or something to lift my spirits.

I found a friend working at a shop, and her day was even worse than mine. As I walked on though, I passed an open-air flower stand with some of the season's first daffodils. Their cheerful sunniness stood out in dramatic contrast to the drippy gray of the streets and the skies. I purchased a half dozen, knowing that they would brighten my room at home.

On the way home, I stopped and gave a couple of them to my friend, hoping to cheer her up. A little bit further along my route, I encountered a light-hearted street person who commented on the flowers. I gave him one too.

At the last corner before my house, there was a shop that I passed nearly every day on my way to and from church and school. My path often crossed with a man who worked there—his big, booming voice a disconcerting contrast to the disabled body in his wheelchair. His greeting was always warm and friendly, but I was intimidated and usually kept my response brief as I hurried on my way.

On this day, my feet took over and I walked past the crosswalk and into the store before my mind had a chance to stop them. I walked up to the counter, and thrust the three remaining daffodils toward him saying, "These are for you, because daffodils are cheerful and you're always cheerful." Still in disbelief at what I had done, I turned and left before he had an opportunity to respond.

I walked home the remaining block a different person. Even though I went without the flowers that I had purchased to cheer myself, the sunshine that came from my heart illuminated my path as though the sun itself had broken through the clouds. The simple act of giving away something that I wanted changed me. I was no longer intimidated by the man at the shop in the corner. I had seen a glimmer that I could be a giving person.

There are many things in Scripture that I don't understand. Things that are so contrary to human nature that it almost seems a mistake that God encourages them. Often we think of what our actions will mean to someone else, but I am sure that God is much more concerned with the effect they have on us. As we learn to give in the way that we see described in this passage, we will see that we benefit far beyond those with whom we share our things.

A Time to Gather

The Lord your God will bless you in all your work.
Deuteronomy 15:10

Brown Bread Ice Cream

This traditional British recipe sounds odd, but the slightly crunchy, nutty flavor of the breadcrumbs is delicious. This is a very simple recipe that doesn't require an ice cream freezer. Brown Bread Ice Cream *can help us keep in mind that working to "earn our keep" can bring sweet rewards.*

2 cups whole wheat bread crumbs

3/4 cup sugar

2 1/2 cups whipping cream

1 teaspoon vanilla extract

1/4 cup confectioners' sugar

In small saucepan, stir breadcrumbs and granulated sugar over low heat. Continue to stir until crumbs are toasted and golden. Be careful not to overcook. Set aside to cool. Break up crumbs while cooling, if necessary.

In large bowl, whip cream, confectioners' sugar and vanilla until thick. Pour into 9-inch square pan and place in freezer. When edges begin to harden (after about 30 minutes), remove from freezer and stir in breadcrumbs.

Return to freezer for at least 4 more hours, stir after each of the first two hours. To retain best flavor, cover with plastic wrap or store in airtight container if not using immediately. *Serve* Brown Bread Ice Cream *with your favorite iced tea.*

A Time to Gather

For you yourselves know how you ought to follow our example. We were not idle when we were with you, nor did we eat anyone's food without paying for it. On the contrary, we worked night and day, laboring and toiling so that we would not be a burden to any of you. We did this, not because we do not have the right to such help, but in order to make ourselves a model for you to follow. For even when we were with you, we gave you this rule: "If a man will not work, he shall not eat."

We hear that some among you are idle. They are not busy; they are busybodies. Such people we command and urge in the Lord Jesus Christ to settle down and earn the bread they eat. And as for you, brothers, never tire of doing what is right.

—2 Thessalonians 3:7–13

When I would read stories in the newspapers about "homeless" beggars who could make several hundred dollars a week panhandling, I always believed that they were a rare exception. And I wanted to believe those signs that said "Will work for food."

Not too long ago though, a local veterans' representative reported that he had tracked down some of the homeless vets that live in a certain part of town. They told him that the services for the homeless were so good that they were very well taken care of and "didn't need to work."

These days it's not just the homeless who don't want to work. College students collect food stamps so they can spend their cash on movies and beer. People go around looking for lawsuits or insurance settlements so they can be "set for life." And every now and then, don't we all have the dream of seeing that prize van pulling up our street to present us with a big check with our names on it?

Of all the Biblical principles we live by, "If a man will not work, he shall not eat," seems easily overlooked.

I've known several people who have had a hard time finding the type of work they really desire or are most qualified to do. But rather than live off the kindness (or duty) of others, they will do jobs that would seem to be "beneath their station" so that no one can say they aren't pulling their own weight. I admire that. So does God.

Even before there was sin, there was work. Work itself was not a curse; the toil and difficulty in accomplishing the work was the curse. It's interesting how our culture focuses so much on retirement, yet it isn't discussed in the Bible as a regular season of life for everyone.

This isn't to say that everyone should have a paying job until they are no longer able to work. I think God is just concerned that we be productive, that we use our time for good purposes. God says that older people can stay busy teaching younger people. Families can care for needy members.

Since much less of our time in this modern world is consumed with actual survival-type work, we have more time that could be spent to help keep kids out of trouble, beautify our city or even help a chosen candidate get elected. Even those among us who have no need to work to support ourselves still need to be productive, contributing members of society.

I think it's important to remember that even at times when we need the help of others, when we need others' assistance for food, clothing or shelter, there is always something we can do to "earn" our way.

If we learn to look at work as more than a necessary evil, and see it rather as the plan that God has for our existence on this earth, we will get much more satisfaction out of the chores that we spend such a large percentage of our time doing. A job well done is pleasing to the Lord and can bring us great satisfaction as well.

I know that there is nothing better for men than to be happy and do good while they live. That everyone may eat and drink, and find satisfaction in all his toil—this is the gift of God.

Ecclesiastes 3:12, 13

A Time to Embrace

You are all one in Christ Jesus.
Galatians 3:28

Poor Man's Cookies

This unusual but simple cookie can help us to remember that just as God does not play favorites among His children, so we should embrace others without favor as well.

3 eggs
1/4 cup milk
1/4 cup sugar
2 3/4 cups flour
1/2 teaspoon salt
vegetable oil for frying
confectioners' sugar for dusting

In large bowl, beat eggs, milk, sugar and salt together. Gradually blend in flour to form soft dough.

Pour dough onto waxed paper, cover and refrigerate for 30 minutes. When chilled, roll dough into a 1/4-inch thick rectangle. With pastry cutter or sharp knife, cut into 3-inch squares.

Cut a slash diagonally across each square. Carefully pull one corner through the slash. Repeat until all dough is used.

In a deep-fat fryer or heavy, deep-sided pan, heat about 2 inches of oil to 375 degrees. Fry dough twists a few at a time for one to two minutes, until golden colored. Turn once or twice to brown on both sides.

Place twists on double thickness of paper towels to drain. When cool, sprinkle with powdered sugar. Poor Man's Cookies *would be good with any of your favorite teas.* 🌿

A Time to Embrace

Suppose a man comes into your meeting wearing a gold ring and fine clothes, and a poor man in shabby clothes also comes in. If you show special attention to the man wearing fine clothes and say, "Here's a good seat for you," but say to the poor man, "You stand there" or "Sit on the floor by my feet," have you not discriminated among yourselves and become judges with evil thoughts?

Listen my dear brothers: Has not God chosen those who are poor in the eyes of the world to be rich in faith and to inherit the kingdom he promised those who love him?

—James 2:2–6

I hardly noticed the man as Dean and I walked to a table in the cafe at our favorite bookstore. He stood at the back of the line, perusing the overhead menu before placing his order. I recognized him as a familiar homeless man—many of the homeless have adopted this bookstore as their new daytime hang out. Coffee is cheap, refills free and you can curl up in a comfortable chair and read all day without anyone really bothering you.

After a few minutes, I got up to take my place in line to order. The shabbily dressed, unkempt, slight man was still at the back of the line. As I approached to take my place behind him, he turned to me as though expecting me to go first. He had been standing there for quite a long time, so I indicated that he should go ahead of me.

The look of surprise on the man's face startled me. I realized that the man must be used to people generally looking past him as though he isn't really there, cutting him off, preventing him from assuming a place in line—or a place in society—that the rest of us take for granted.

It brought tears to my eyes to realize how often we can diminish the value of other people because they aren't dressed as nicely as we are, or they don't speak the language as well as we do, or they pay for their coffee with money they've collected by recycling soda cans.

Abigail Van Buren, America's "Dear Abby," said, "The best index to a person's character is how he treats people who can't do him any good and how he treats people who can't fight back."

This isn't true just in the twentieth century. The early church needed to be reminded that God hadn't shown favoritism to them, and they in turn should embrace others. Jesus himself set an example of compassion toward the poor and "lowly." God has always instructed his children to be merciful toward the poor and otherwise unfortunate.

It's not just the poor who are treated differently anymore. It can be people with different points of view—political, theological or social. We insulate ourselves from everyone who seems different, and when we do encounter them, it's as though they aren't really a part of the family.

It's not enough to look at the poor or elderly as "ministry opportunities." Of course it's great to help meet people's needs, but beyond feeding them or giving them our cast-off clothing, we need to treat those people with the same respect and humanity we offer anyone we view as our equals.

Jesus was often criticized for associating with people who were considered "lowly," but a large part of his ministry was spent showing that people aren't valuable to God because of their wealth, status or religion. It is faith and a willingness to follow Christ that God values most.

What a blessing it is to realize that God himself accepts us without favor. If God values all people and even sent Christ to "preach the Gospel to the poor" (Luke 4:18), we should also exhibit that attitude toward others. Let's rejoice in God's great, unconditional acceptance of us and show our gratitude by extending acceptance to all those we encounter.

You are all sons of God through faith in Christ Jesus . . .
There is neither Jew nor Greek, slave nor free, male nor female,
for you are all one in Christ Jesus.

Galatians 3:26, 28

A Time to Give Up

Store up for yourselves treasures in heaven.
Matthew 6:20

Treasure Cookies

These American cookies, with their abundance of rich treats, are a "treasure" of a cookie. They're sure to disappear so quickly they'll be a reminder that what we invest in here on earth is only temporary—but we can find ways to make eternal investments.

1 1/2 cups graham cracker crumbs

1/2 cup butter

1 cup butterscotch or peanut butter chips

1 cup semi-sweet chocolate chips

1 cup pecans or walnuts, chopped

1/2 cup flaked coconut (optional)

1 jar (7-ounce) marshmallow creme

Preheat oven to 375 degrees. Lightly grease 9x13-inch baking pan.

In medium bowl, mix graham cracker crumbs with butter; stir to mix thoroughly. Spread mixture evenly over bottom of baking pan.

In medium bowl, mix together all chips and nuts. Add marshmallow creme and stir until well mixed.

Spread mixture evenly over crust. If desired, sprinkle coconut over top. Bake 25 to 30 minutes and until nuts appear toasted and golden. Cool in pan before cutting into squares with sharp knife. Treasure Cookies *are so rich that they are best served with a strong black tea like English or Irish Breakfast tea.*

A Time to Give Up

Do not store up for yourselves treasures on earth, where moth and rust destroy, and where thieves break in and steal. But store up for yourselves treasures in heaven, where moth and rust do not destroy, and where thieves do not break in and steal. For where your treasure is, there your heart will be also.

—Matthew 6:19–21

Our trusty Datsun 280Z had more than 300,000 miles on its original engine when Dean and I were rear-ended by a truck. Rather than put the settlement money back into the twenty-year-old sports car, we "splurged" and bought a ten-year-old British car—a Sterling. It was probably a luxury car when it was new, but after being very definitely broken in for years, most of the luxury had been worn away. Even so, with four doors that actually locked, air conditioning that worked and no exhaust leaks, it was still a definite step up for us.

In the first couple of weeks the Sterling was in the shop more than in our driveway—getting belts changed and the transmission adjusted. Just when the repairs seemed to be over with, it somehow wandered out of our driveway, made a perfect U-turn and backed into a neighbor's Winnebago!

It was hard to find any humor or meaning in the situation, although the irony was evident—if you like irony. It took several weeks to get things settled and to get the car fixed. Those weeks of driving the scarred car did make me look at it differently. Now, even though it looks better than it did when we got it, it's just a comfortable car that gets us around. Not to over-spiritualize a freak accident, but even though the Sterling was no treasure, the incident was a subtle reminder not to get too attached to earthly things.

What is your treasure? A special collection? Family heirlooms? Precious jewelry or valuable artwork? Maybe your work is your treasure—maybe what you do and who you are as a result gives you identity and security.

I do love to have beautiful things around. Our appreciation for beauty certainly comes from the Lord. God loves beauty, too. It shows in the descriptions of the tabernacle and temple and the grandeur in which God wanted to reside. God even appreciates people's ability to craft things—I'm sure He is pleased by things we make ourselves and the work we do. But

He also warns us against putting too much energy into accumulating things here on earth.

I think sometimes when we get something that means a lot to us, we act almost like little children. Everything is precious to a small child still discovering the world around him—even bugs and caterpillars and other creepy-crawly things. Children often hold a new treasure tightly to make sure it doesn't escape their grasp. It's not usually too long before they learn that a tight grasp can bring about the very result they feared. The flattened flower no longer looks so pretty and the crushed caterpillar no longer tickles their cheek. Eventually a child will learn that if she holds the treasure with an open hand, she can delight in the beauty and enjoy the uniqueness of it.

We need to learn to do that. To hold our treasure with an open hand that allows us to appreciate and enjoy it but won't break our hearts or cause us great pain if it is somehow lost.

Everything in this life is temporary. The treasures we accumulate, the things we accomplish, even our relationships with those we love. Although we may all be together again in eternity, it won't be the same as it is now.

So what should we be doing?

"Storing up treasures in heaven."

That may mean sharing what you know about God with others in your life so that they might be with Him one day as well. Perhaps it means learning to pray more deeply and gain new insights into God's Word so that you know Him more intimately and your relationship with Him becomes a new treasure to you. Maybe it is learning to sing or play an instrument that allows you to worship Him in a new way.

Ultimately, it means spending time doing whatever it is that turns our focus away from this temporary, trivial world and turns it to our beloved Lord with whom we have all of eternity to reap the benefits of our investment.

Enjoy the beauty of this world. God gave it to you.

Be a good steward of the blessings and riches He has allowed you to possess.

But most of all, be sure that the things that mean the most to you are the ones that will bring eternal joy and satisfaction.

Set your mind on things above, not on earthly things.

Colossians 3:2

A Time to Keep

I will be a Father to you.
2 Corinthians 6:18

Homestead Cookies

This simple American cookie keeps and travels well. It is said to get its name from traveling west across the United States with the homesteaders. Homestead Cookies *can help us remember God cares for us in our loneliness.*

1 cup flour

2 cups rolled oats

1/2 teaspoon baking powder

1/2 teaspoon baking soda

1/2 teaspoon salt

1 cup apples, chopped fine

1/2 cup (1 stick) butter, soft but not melted

1/2 cup sugar

1/2 cup light brown sugar, packed

1 egg

1 teaspoon vanilla extract

Preheat oven to 375 degrees. Line baking sheets with parchment or grease lightly.

In large bowl, cream together butter, granulated sugar and brown sugar until light and fluffy. Beat in egg and vanilla extract.

In another bowl, stir together flour, oats, baking powder, baking soda and salt.

Gradually mix dry ingredients into butter mixture. Stir in apples.

Drop about a tablespoonful of dough onto prepared baking sheets, leaving 1 1/2 inches between them.

Bake for 8 to 10 minutes or until light golden. Cool on wire racks, store in airtight container. Homestead Cookies *freeze well and are delicious served with cinnamon or apple-flavored tea.*

A Time to Keep

A father to the fatherless, a defender of the widows,
  is God in his holy dwelling.
God sets the lonely in families,
  he leads forth the prisoners with singing;
  but the rebellious live in a sun-scorched land.

—Psalm 68:5–6

The lonely and left-behind are often overlooked in the world today—even in the church. Yet throughout Scripture, God tells His people to look after orphans and widows. More than that, God promises to be their support and protector.

A young widow was doing her best to raise her son on her own. She involved Tommy in church activities that would bring men into his life. One group had an annual Father-Son Soapbox Derby. Bill, a neighbor who helped lead the group, offered to be Tommy's cheering section since he had no son.

The rules said that the boys had to do most of the work on the carts themselves. Mom helped choose the paint and come up with the basic shape of the cart, but Tommy did the rest.

The big day arrived with great anticipation. Bill had to help set up for the event, so Tommy and his mother carefully loaded his cart into the van and drove to the park to meet Bill. As they arrived at the park, the scene was a jumble of boys, their dads and colorful soapbox carts that had fancy shapes and elaborate paint jobs—well beyond the capabilities of the eight-year-olds proudly displaying them.

As Tommy dejectedly unloaded his rough-hewn, childishly painted cart, he said, "I wish I had a dad." It was hard for his mom to know what to say. She wished he had a dad—and she a husband, too.

Rather than expressing her sadness and frustration though, she took him gently in her arms and said, "Darling, you do have a Father. You have a Heavenly Father who loves you and has always looked after you. He will never let you down."

Tommy wasn't completely convinced, but he took his cart and met Bill at the starting area.

The race went in stages: three carts competing against each other with the winner of each race later competing against other winners. Tommy's cart was the fastest in his first race, then again in two more races to take first place in his age group. Then there was a race among the winners of the youngest students—Tommy won again.

The final race was among the winners of each age group—the winner would be the fastest among all the boys there. Tommy's little-boy craftsmanship and paint job didn't slow him down at all—his cart was the fastest of them all!

When Bill dropped Tommy at home, he bounced through the door with excitement, "Mom! I really do have a Father!" He got down on his knees and thanked God for being the best dad a kid could have.

Although it's difficult at times not having the actual physical presence of a person to comfort and help us, we can have confidence that the hands of God will hold us close in ways that no earthly friend ever could.

Whether you are widowed or never married, orphaned or abandoned, lost or simply lonely, you have a Father ... Lover ... Friend ... and Home ... in heaven. God's as near as you'll allow Him to be.

> *"I will be a Father to you, and you will be my sons and daughters, says the Lord Almighty."*
>
> 2 Corinthians 6:18

A Time to be Silent

Lips that speak knowledge are a rare jewel.
Proverbs 20:15

Queen Cakes

I don't know if these get their name because they were a favorite of one of the queens of England or simply because they are fit for a queen. Queen Cakes *can help us to remember that restraint is a "royal" trait.*

1/4 cup currants

1/2 cup (1 stick) butter or margarine

1/2 cup sugar

3/4 cup flour

1 teaspoon baking powder

2 eggs

Preheat oven to 350 degrees. In small bowl, add 1 teaspoon of flour to currants and toss till coated. Set aside.

In medium bowl, cream together butter and sugar. Sift together flour and baking powder. Add to creamed mixture a little at a time, alternating with eggs. Stir until smooth. Stir in currants.

Butter cups of muffin tins or fluted brioche molds and spoon batter into them, filling about 1/2 full.

Bake for 15 to 20 minutes until golden or until a toothpick inserted in center comes out clean. Queen Cakes *are delicious with orange-flavored tea.*

A Time to be Silent

When the king's order and edict had been proclaimed, many girls were brought to the citadel of Susa, and put under the care of Hegai. Esther also was taken to the king's palace, and entrusted to Hegai, who had charge of the harem. The girl pleased him, and won his favor . . .

Esther had not revealed her nationality and family background, because Mordecai (her guardian) had forbidden her to do so. Every day he walked back and forth near the courtyard of the harem to find out how Esther was and what was happening to her.

Before a girl's turn came to go in to King Xerxes, she had to complete twelve months of beauty treatments. . . . and this is how she would go to the king: Anything she wanted was given her to take with her from the harem to the king's palace. . . . When the turn came for Esther (the girl Mordecai had adopted, the daughter of his uncle Abihail) to go to the king, she asked for nothing other than what Hegai, the king's eunuch who was in charge of the harem, suggested. And Esther won the favor of everyone who saw her. . . . Now the king was attracted to Esther more than any of the other women, and she won his favor and approval more than any of the other virgins. So he set a royal crown on her head and made her queen instead of Vashti.

—Esther 2:8–17

What would you do if you learned that your family was going to be killed? Would you write a letter to the editor of the newspaper to alert the community? Maybe call together all your relatives to protest? Mobilize a petition drive and notify the media? Call the church prayer chain?

Esther is an example of how exercising restraint can help you to get what is really important. Esther was given the opportunity to ask for anything she wanted. She had been wisely counseled to ask for little. This became critical later on when what she really needed was something so big that she knew she might lose her own life just by asking for it.

The book of Esther goes on to tell of how the king's right-hand man, Haman, wanted to destroy all the Jews because Mordecai wouldn't violate his religion and kneel before Haman. Because he was trusted by the king, Haman had the authority to make decrees and carry them out.

Esther didn't immediately run to the king to expose Haman's plan and demand justice. She carefully earned the respect of the king and the right to be heard. When she revealed the plan to destroy the Jews, the king saved Esther and her people and even gave her cousin Mordecai the job that Haman had held and made him ruler over Haman's house.

I think if Esther had been one to make frequent demands of the king, like the little boy who cried "Wolf!", her message that her people were to be destroyed might have fallen on deaf ears.

Restraint is not a quality that is highly prized in America. In fact, Americans seem to be known in other cultures for our brashness and willingness to say whatever is on our minds.

Often we make excuses for speaking our mind: it's an important issue others need to be informed about; a wrong has been done and attention must be called to it; someone has been "getting away with" something and he needs to be stopped.

Although the saying is "the squeaky wheel gets the grease," it's important to note that the goal is to silence the wheel. The grease isn't given out of fondness or affection, it's simply to shut it up.

The Bible speaks more about remaining silent when wronged than it does about standing up for ourselves. The most profound example of this was Christ himself: " . . . as a sheep before her shearers is silent so he did not open his mouth." (Isaiah 53:7)

As Josh Billing put it, "The best time for you to hold your tongue is the time you feel you must say something or bust." Although it runs contrary to our culture, we should be aware that there is a right time and place for expressing our opinions and concerns. Whether it's something at work, at church or even at home, it's important to pick our platforms carefully and exercise restraint even when the battle is ours to fight.

> " . . . *A woman of understanding holds her tongue.*"
> Proverbs 11:12b

A Time to Speak

Be very careful, then, how you live—not as unwise but as wise, making the most of every opportunity.

Ephesians 5:15, 16

Fresh Cranberry Fool

This simple British dessert is typically made with gooseberries, but cranberries or red currants have the same tart taste that's required for an authentic fool. Serve it as a reminder that our actions often speak louder than our words—even when we haven't said we're followers of Christ, we're not fooling anyone.

12 ounces cranberries (fresh, or frozen and thawed)

2 tablespoons butter

1/4 cup sugar

1 pint heavy cream

Melt butter over low heat in heavy saucepan. Add cranberries and sugar. Cook berries in covered pan over lowest heat until soft and mushy.

Remove from heat and stir berries until thoroughly mashed. Put through fine mesh sieve, discarding skins and seeds. If berries are too tart, add another tablespoon or two of sugar. Set aside to cool completely.

When berries are cooled, whip cream until fluffy and fairly stiff. Gently fold in cranberries. Spoon into glass serving dishes or goblets. Refrigerate for at least one hour before serving. *A fruit fool is another treat that goes well with iced tea—try something with mint or orange flavoring.*

A Time to Speak

Simon Peter and another disciple were following Jesus. Because this disciple was known to the high priest, he went with Jesus into the high priest's courtyard, but Peter had to wait outside at the door. The other disciple, who was known to the high priest, came back, spoke to the girl on duty there and brought Peter in.

"You are not one of his disciples, are you?" the girl at the door asked Peter.

He replied, "I am not."

It was cold, and the servants and officials stood around a fire they had made to keep warm. Peter also was standing with them, warming himself.

As Simon Peter stood warming himself, he was asked, "You are not one of his disciples, are you?"

He denied it, saying, "I am not."

One of the high priest's servants, a relative of the man whose ear Peter had cut off, challenged him, "Didn't I see you with him in the olive grove?" Again Peter denied it, and at that moment a rooster began to crow.

—John 18:15–18, 25–27

Have you ever driven a sports car? Some cars really do seem to "enjoy" going fast. I find it hard not to drive a sports car like a sports car: be the first person "off the line" when the light changes; get up to maximum speed as quickly as possible; easily get around slow-moving trucks.

When we were first married, our only car was a 1975 Datsun 280z—a "persimmon"–colored sports car with a bicycle rack on top and a slight dent in the front end. (Not exactly inconspicuous.)

A few months after our wedding, my husband was asked to teach the college group at our church. It was a large group, more than a hundred students, and I didn't know very many of them. It was a fairly small town, and I knew that I could encounter students from the church at just about any time without being aware of it. For the most part, this wasn't a problem, but I realized there was one area that could get me into trouble—my driving.

I felt convicted that I should tone things down so I wouldn't cause any problems for Dean in his new position. I was afraid that it could reflect badly on Dean if any of his students saw me zipping around town when I wasn't aware of them.

At the same moment I came to that realization, I remembered that even before Dean was asked to teach—in fact, long before we were married—I had made another commitment, and part of that commitment was to bring Christ honor and glory rather than dishonor. I realized that I shouldn't take security in what I perceive as "anonymity." I am always a follower of Christ, and that should always show.

We've all heard that "actions speak louder than words." It's estimated that as much as eighty percent of communication is non-verbal. As Peter saw, sometimes we don't have to tell people that we're followers of Christ. If we live right, it should show.

Writer and speaker Joanne Wallace tells of being at Chicago's O'Hare International Airport trying to make a connection in order to get home in time to lead a seminar for people coming from all over the country. She felt a lot of responsibility toward the group, and much pressure to arrive on time. She had missed one flight and encountered some trouble at the ticket counter trying to get another.

Joanne remembers that she wanted to say, "Don't you know who I am?" thinking maybe her celebrity status might get things to work more smoothly for her. But she resisted the temptation, got her ticket, and went off to wait the three hours until her flight.

After writing a few notes and looking in the airport gift shops, she went to the coffee shop. She was surprised when the ticket agent who had helped her approached her table.

"Excuse me, Mrs. Wallace, I know who you are—I saw you on a Christian television program. I've been looking into Christianity for awhile. I see the preachers and other Christians on TV, and then I see them come here to catch their planes. Like I said, I've been looking into Christianity for awhile, and I was watching you. Thank you for not letting me down." He turned and left a speechless Joanne silently thanking God that she hadn't blown it. Joanne says she hasn't been the same since—you never know who's looking at you as an example of Christ.

Just like Peter was recognized as a follower of Christ, people will know it of us whether we tell them or not. We should remember that our actions will confirm what our words sometimes won't admit. We need to take care that our "body language" is telling people what we want it to.

A Time to Love

You are a letter from Christ.
2 Corinthians 3:3

Love Letters

These cookies, with their pastry crust shaped like an envelope and sweet filling, can be a reminder of the sweet influence we can have in the world as God's "Letters of Love."

Crust

Use the pastry recipe from Half Moon Cookies (pg. 25) or your own favorite short-crust recipe or purchased pie dough, enough for 2 nine-inch deep dish pies.

Filling

2 egg whites

1/4 cup sugar

1/2 teaspoon ground cinnamon

1 cup blanched almonds, finely ground

1 teaspoon grated lemon zest

To make filling, beat egg whites in a medium bowl until stiff peaks form. Do not overbeat. Stir in sugar and cinnamon. Fold in almonds and lemon zest. Set aside. Preheat oven to 350 degrees.

On lightly floured surface, roll dough to 1/4-inch thick rectangle. Using pastry wheel or sharp knife, cut into 3-inch squares.

Place 1-inch apart on ungreased baking sheets. Put a teaspoonful of filling in the center of each square. Lightly brush edges with remaining egg white, draw corners of dough into center, overlapping the top flap like an envelope. Press seams lightly to seal.

Bake for 18 to 20 minutes until light golden colored. Cool on wire racks. Store in airtight container. Love Letters *go nicely with lemon or rose-flavored tea.* 🌸

A Time to Love

Are we beginning to commend ourselves again? Or do we need, like some people, letters of recommendation to you or from you? You yourselves are our letter, written on our hearts, known and read by everybody. You show that you are a letter from Christ, the result of our ministry, written not with ink but with the Spirit of the living God, not on tablets of stone but on tablets of human hearts.

Such confidence as this is ours through Christ before God. Not that we are competent in ourselves to claim anything for ourselves, but our competence comes from God. He has made us competent as ministers of a new covenant—not of the letter but of the Spirit; for the letter kills, but the Spirit gives life.

Did you know that you and I are God's love letters to the world? We are letters of the Spirit of God. As Paul says, the Spirit gives life. You never know what small kindness will demonstrate love to someone.

—2 Corinthians 3:1–6

In the mid–1980s American missionaries living in Washington, D.C. wanted to have guests for the Thanksgiving holiday. They discussed whom to invite, agreeing that it should be someone who wouldn't be likely to have another invitation. They decided to invite the Libyan ambassadors, knowing that the conflict between the U.S. and Libya made anyone connected with Libya very unpopular.

The Libyans accepted the invitation and enjoyed the traditional American celebration. "No one has invited us to anything since we've been here," they told their hosts. "If there is ever anything we can do for you, please let us know."

The comment was forgotten until the missionaries found themselves traveling through the Middle East. They decided to see if they could arrange for a visit with Mohmar Khadafi, the greatly disliked and much-feared leader of the Libyan conflict. The ambassador did not sound hopeful that such a meeting could be arranged—Khadafi was not known for being accessible or welcoming, but he promised to see what he could do.

When the Americans arrived at the airport, they received word that the Libyan leader agreed to meet them for fifteen minutes. Although they were somewhat nervous, they knew they were going in the strength of the Lord and that He would bless their efforts and protect them.

Khadafi's English was very good, so there was no communication barrier. In fact, the leader had been educated in the United States. He told the missionaries that as a lonely student in America, no one ever included him in parties or activities. It was a source of his dislike for Americans in general.

At that point the missionary said, "I would like to pray for you right now." So the group bowed their heads and the missionary prayed that Khadafi would lead righteously and justly. At the conclusion of the prayer, Khadafi told the missionary that no one, not even his own religious advisors, had ever prayed for him that way. He called for a photographer to take a picture of the group. For many years after, that photo ran at the conclusion of television broadcasting each day until the morning. God's love had been demonstrated once again by men willing to reach beyond themselves and offer hope to those who needed it.

Ann Kiemel Anderson has lived that way. Her books are filled with examples of occasions when she took a deep breath and shared God's love with someone in the next seat on an airplane, a clerk at a store, a lonely child in the neighborhood. After one airplane encounter, her new friend said, "Ann, I never have had anyone love me the way you defined it, . . ." As Ann said goodbye, she assured him that one day he would know what love is. She later received a letter that said, " . . . for the first time I really believed God is . . ."

You and I can do the same thing for people we meet. Just as Paul and the other early apostles left a legacy among the believers in the early church, and they in turn reached the entire world, so can we who are willing to be used also impart a legacy of Christ's love in the lives of those we encounter. As the old saying goes, "You may be the only Bible someone ever reads."

We always thank God for all of you, mentioning you in our prayers. We continually remember before our God and Father your work produced by faith, your labor prompted by love, and your endurance inspired by hope in our Lord Jesus Christ.

1 Thessalonians 1:2–3

A Time for Peace

It shall be a jubilee for you.
Leviticus 25:10

Jubilee Wafers

Jubilee Wafers *are very similar to a traditional Swedish Spice Cookie. The lively celebration of flavors in these cookies can be a reminder to take time off when you need to bring a measure of peace into your life.*

2/3 cup honey
1/2 cup firmly packed brown sugar
1/2 cup (1 stick) unsalted butter
2 cups flour
1 teaspoon baking powder
1/2 teaspoon baking soda
1 teaspoon ground cinnamon
1/2 teaspoon ground cloves

1/2 teaspoon ground nutmeg
1/4 teaspoon ground cardamom
  or allspice
1 cup finely chopped, blanched
  almonds
Finely grated rind of 2 oranges
1 teaspoon almond extract or
  rum extract

In medium saucepan, stir honey, brown sugar and butter over medium heat. Stir until sugar is dissolved and ingredients are blended. Remove from heat and set aside to cool.

In large bowl, mix together flour, baking soda and spices. When honey mixture is cooled to lukewarm, stir in extract.

Stir honey mixture into dry ingredients. Add chopped almonds and orange rind. Divide dough into 2 logs, 2 inches in diameter. Wrap in waxed paper or plastic wrap and refrigerate for about 30 minutes.

Preheat oven to 350 degrees. Lightly grease baking sheets with butter or line with parchment paper.

Using sharp knife, cut logs into 1/4-inch thick slices. Place 1 inch apart on baking sheets. Bake for 12 to 15 minutes or until set.

Cool on wire racks. Store in airtight containers. Jubilee Wafers *are good with cinnamon-orange tea or your favorite iced tea.* 🌿

A Time for Peace

"'Count off seven sabbaths of years—seven times seven years—so that the seven sabbaths of years amount to a period of forty nine years. Then have the trumpet sounded everywhere on the tenth day of the seventh month; on the Day of Atonement sound the trumpet throughout your land. Consecrate the fiftieth year and proclaim liberty throughout the land to all its inhabitants. It shall be a jubilee for you; each one of you is to return to his family property and each to his own clan.'"
—Leviticus 25:8–10

Jubilee is an example of an Old Testament celebration that we no longer observe. I think that if we look at Jubilee though, we'll see that there is much we can learn from these traditions that can enrich our lives today.

Jubilee was a time of peace and freedom: a time when slaves were released, property returned to the original owner and forgiveness was given to family members or others in debt. It was a time to remember that God was the actual owner of everything.

In addition to the physical involvement of returning land and reuniting with family, it was also a time of spiritual renewal. Time off from the usual work of planting and harvesting to focus on what God had done and to renew that relationship.

Now that we live under grace, the traditions God set up are no longer commands, but I believe we can still benefit from keeping the spirit of the traditions alive.

My friend Vicky Kuyper recently had a "Jubilee" of her own. Since she was a little girl she had wanted to hike Machupichu in Peru. A friend who was turning 40 wanted to take a boat down the Amazon. They combined their dreams and took the trip together. Things didn't go quite as planned—rather than staying at the resort they signed up for, Vicky and her friend got placed in a type of survival camp instead. It was no luxury vacation, but Vicky said it was the greatest experience of her life.

She's been a wife, mother, writer, and friend for so long that she couldn't remember when she had last been "just Vicky." She said, "Throughout the trip, everywhere I looked there was a parable from God to me." Leaving behind family, friends, commitments and reputation, Vicky was alone with God for the first time in a long time. And while it was a wonderful experience, it wasn't as though she wanted to stay there. She came back stronger, closer to God, and more focused on what is important in her life. That's what Jubilee is about.

The spirit of Jubilee can be kept in our own hearts and lives even though it is no longer a community event. Whether you are a woman nearing your own fiftieth "Jubilee Year," or you have passed the Jubilee, or maybe you are yet to reach the Sabbath of Sabbaths in your own life, bringing the traits of the Jubilee into your life can be an enriching experience.

Jubilee was time set apart. When was the last time you took time off from extra commitments at church or with community organizations? Today, we often have difficulty finding time to set apart a weekend or a vacation, let alone an entire year. Maybe we can modify that to work Jubilee into our schedules.

Since this is a symbolic Jubilee we're talking about, I'd like to think maybe we could take stock in this way every 50th month, rather than every 50th year. At the start of every fifth year, you could take a break from commitments to church activities or charities to refocus and prioritize. It could be a couple of weeks or several months. Time that was previously spent at meetings could be used to spend special time with family. Possessions could be reduced or closets cleaned out to give things to charity. You could begin a spiritual journal to record the little lessons that God shows you and dedicate special time to begin a new study of the character of God or attend a conference or retreat to renew your spiritual life.

Jubilee can be a time that we cut back on our commitments so we can focus on the things God recommended: focus on family—both ancestors and offspring; unburden ourselves of possessions; take time off from "work" to worship God and see what He's done for us. I think we'll find a refreshed spirit and be ready to start a new phase of life with greater peace and contentment.

It is for freedom that Christ has set us free. Stand firm, then, and do not let yourselves be burdened again by a yoke of slavery.

Galatians 5:1

In Conclusion ... Keep His Commandments

How sweet are your words to my taste.
Psalm 119:103

Honey Cream Cookies

Serve these cookies as a reminder that the Word of God is sweeter than honey to the taste and more desirable than gold.

1/2 cup butter or shortening	*Filling*
1 cup honey	2 oz. cream cheese
2 1/2 cups flour	1 tablespoon honey
1 teaspoon baking soda	2 cups powdered sugar
1 teaspoon ginger or cardamom	
1 teaspoon salt	

In large saucepan, melt together butter or shortening and honey, stirring until smooth. In medium bowl, combine flour, baking soda, ginger and salt.

Gradually blend dry ingredients into honey mixture, stirring until a smooth dough is formed. Refrigerate until firm.

When ready to bake, preheat oven to 350 degrees. Grease baking sheets or cover with parchment.

Flour work surface and rolling pin. Roll dough to 1/4 to 1/8-inch thickness. Cut into rounds and place 1 inch apart on prepared baking sheets. Bake for 12–14 minutes or until light golden in color.

Cool on wire racks.

While cookies cool, blend cream cheese and honey. Add powdered sugar and blend until a stiff icing is formed. When cookies are completely cooled, place about 1/2 teaspoon of icing in center of bottom side of one cookie. Cover icing with another cookie and press together gently to form a sandwich.

To retain crispness, store cookies in airtight container as soon as they are filled. Honey Cream Cookies *are great with honey or almond-flavored teas.*

In Conclusion . . . Keep His Commandments

The law of the Lord is perfect, reviving the soul.
The statutes of the Lord are trustworthy, making wise the simple.
The precepts of the Lord are right, giving joy to the heart.
The commands of the Lord are radiant, giving light to the eyes.
The fear of the Lord is pure, enduring forever.
The ordinances of the Lord are sure and altogether righteous.
They are more precious than gold, than much pure gold;
they are sweeter than honey, than honey from the comb.

Oh, how I love your law!
 I meditate on it all day long.
You commands make me wiser than my enemies,
 for they are ever with me.
I have more insight than all my teachers,
 for I meditate on your statutes.
I have more understanding than the elders,
 for I obey your precepts.
I have kept my feet from every evil path
 so that I might obey your word.
I have not departed from your laws, for you yourself have taught me.
How sweet are your words to my taste,
 sweeter than honey to my mouth!

—Psalm 19:7–10; Psalm 119:97–103

My friends Mark and Rhonda had one of the most special and unique weddings I have ever attended. Mark planned the ceremony, choosing the words to be spoken very carefully. It was the only wedding I remember where the words that the bride and groom spoke to one another were words of Scripture. They were committing to one another in Christ—what better words of commitment than the words of God himself? Surely the Author of love and marriage has expressed it far better than any of us could!

Have you ever been in church and heard the minister give a message, but found you got something different from it than someone else who heard the same sermon? It's not because you heard the preacher differently, but because the word of God has the power to touch us in whatever our circumstances.

What sets the Bible apart from all other books is the Author. God wrote the Bible using human hands and words to communicate with you and me in a tangible, real way. It's like a personal letter from God to you—to me.

My husband has written two words in the front of his Bible to remind him of this. The inscription reads, "Dear Dean . . ." Whenever studying the Bible becomes routine, he reminds himself that he is holding a personal message from God—what a precious thing! It's great that a preacher can explain the historical context of Scripture and introduce us to new thoughts or insights, but it would still be productive if he did nothing other than stand and read from God's word for the entire service.

That is why I've included whole portions of Scripture in this book rather than just a reference and my thoughts on the topic. God's words are so precious, why skimp? If this book had to be reduced by half, or you could only read a portion of each devotion, I would rather you skip my words and anecdotes and read only the portions of Scripture.

Dr. J. Vernon McGee had a special love for God's word. For many years he hosted the radio program "Through the Bible." Even though he went home to be with the Lord several years ago, his program is still on the air. Dr. McGee didn't just preach a sermon, but read large portions of Scripture on each show. It was formatted so he preached and read through the entire Bible every 5 years.

My former pastor tells of visiting Dr. McGee during his last days on earth. He no longer recognized the people who came to see him and couldn't carry on a conversation with those in the room. At first it appeared that Dr. McGee was talking in his sleep, but as they drew near enough to hear, what they heard was preaching! Even in his sleep, Dr. McGee's words were the words of God that he loved so dearly.

The English preacher R.C. Chapman said, "There are mysteries of grace and love in the Bible: it is a thriving soul that finds the Book of God growing more and more precious." May God's words always be the most precious words in your heart.

My soul is consumed with longing for your laws at all times.
Psalm 119:20

Thank you Apple Farm!

*T*he photography for *A Tea for All Seasons* was taken at **The Apple Farm** in Central California. Its beautiful country gardens and Victorian-styled decor served as a fitting backdrop to Mary Pielenz Hampton's tea recipes and devotionals. The author and editors are especially grateful for the careful attention of the owners and staff of this four-diamond inn, restaurant, mill, and gift shop.

As unique as the teatime experiences contained in this book, this charming retreat provides guests with a quiet place away from their daily routines to find a time of refreshment. Owners Katy and Bob Davis welcome guests to enjoy the quaint surroundings of their gracious restaurant, a picnic lunch, or to relax with a sumptuous and leisurely breakfast in bed.

The Apple Farm is located in San Luis Obispo, California and can be conveniently reached from U.S. highway 101. Our sincere thanks to one of California's hidden treasures!

Notes

1. M. Dalton King, *Special Teas* (New York: Kenan Books, 1993).

2. Carole Manchester, *French Tea: The Pleasures of the Table* (New York: Hearst Books, 1993).

3. A.W. Tozer, *The Knowledge of the Holy* (New York: Harper Collins Press, 1992).

4. George Muller, *The Autobiography of George Muller* (Springdale, PA.: Whitaker House, 1984).

5. Dr. E.C. Krupp, *Beyond the Blue Horizon* (Cambridge, England: Oxford University Press, 1992).

6. Sara Stein, *Noah's Garden* (New York: Houghton Mifflin Co.,1993).

7. Evelyn H. Lauder, *Seasons Observed* (New York: Harry N. Abrams, 1994).

8. Charles Swindoll, *Growing Strong in the Seasons of Life* (Sisters, OR.: Multnomah Press, 1984).

9. Joan Wester Anderson, *Where Miracles Happen* (New York:Ballantine Books, 1994).

10. Oswald Chambers, *He Shall Glorify Me* (Ft. Washington, PA.: Christian Literature Crusade, 1965).

11. Michael Card, *Parable of Joy* (Nashville, TN.: Thomas Nelson Publishers, 1995).

12. George Sweeting, *Great Quotes and Illustrations* (Dallas:Word, Inc., 1985).

13. Ann Kiemel Anderson, *I Love the Word Impossible* (Wheaton, Ill.: Tyndale House Publishers, 1976).

14. Robert L. Peterson & Alexander Strauch, *Agape Leadership* (Littleton, CO.: Lewis & Roth Publishers, 1991).

The author would like to express her gradidude to the following companies for their generous contribution of articles used in the photography. All businesses are located in San Luis Obispo, CA.

The Boxworks
Time 'n Treasures
Forden's
Country Classics
Daylight Gardens
The Parable

MONSIEUR PAMPLEMOUSSE ALOFT

MONSIEUR PAMPLEMOUSSE
MONSIEUR PAMPLEMOUSSE AND THE SECRET MISSION
MONSIEUR PAMPLEMOUSSE ON THE SPOT
MONSIEUR PAMPLEMOUSSE TAKES THE CURE

MONSIEUR PAMPLEMOUSSE ALOFT

MICHAEL BOND

FAWCETT COLUMBINE • NEW YORK

A Fawcett Columbine Book
Published by Ballantine Books

Copyright © Michael Bond 1989

Library of Congress Cataloging-in-Publication Data

Bond, Michael.
    Monsieur Pamplemousse aloft / Michael Bond.—1st
American ed.
        p.   cm.
    ISBN 0-449-90455-5 : $14.95
    I. Title
PR6052.052M67   1989
823'.914—dc20   89-90819
                                                 CIP

Manufactured in the United States of America

First American Edition: September 1989

10 9 8 7 6 5 4 3 2 1

CONTENTS

1

SOMETHING IN THE AIR

Pommes Frites saw it first; a small object shaped like a sausage and about the size of a double magnum of champagne. Its silver body gleamed in the early morning sun as it emerged from the comparative gloom of the Boulevard de la Tour-Maubourg in the seventh *arrondissement* of Paris and entered the Place de Santiago-du-Chili. Gliding along at roof-top level, it disappeared for a moment or two behind some trees, nosed its way slowly and silently along one side of the *Place*, eventually reappearing outside the Chilean Embassy on the corner of the Avenue de la Motte-Picquet. There it paused in its travels, gaining height momentarily, as though trying to discover what secrets lay behind the façade of the white stone building. Then, curiosity apparently satisfied, it executed a sharp 270-degree turn to port and went on its way again, following a course running parallel to the outer wall of the Hôtel des Invalides, home amongst other things, to the remains of the Emperor Napoleon.

Pommes Frites' immediate reaction on catching sight of it had been one of incredulity; incredulity which quickly gave way to apprehension. He still had vivid memories of a recent journey he had undertaken in the Pyrénées Orientales suspended beneath his inflatable kennel. It had been an unhappy experience and one he had no wish to repeat. Gathering himself together, he gave vent to a warning howl, vaguely, but in the circumstances not inaptly, reminiscent of an air-raid siren.

However, to have awarded Pommes Frites bonus points for his powers of observation would have been doing less than justice to those others who were abroad that morning. It was barely nine-thirty and most passers-by had their minds on other, more pressing matters – like getting to work on time. The overalled worker in the tiny triangular railed-in park outside the Metro station was busy watering his roses, while the taxi-drivers waiting in a line nearby had their eyes firmly fixed on lower horizons.

The truth of the matter was, Pommes Frites only happened to strike lucky because, having raced on ahead of his master, he alone in the Place de Santiago-du-Chili was gazing up at the statue of Vauban just as the object floated past. Not many, other than those with a passion for history, paused to give the statue so much as a passing glance at the best of times, and Pommes Frites was only looking at it for want of something better to do while bestowing his favours on a convenient tree. Far from centering his thoughts on the past exploits of one of France's most famous military engineers, he was wondering idly whether, if he kept very still, a pigeon perched on top of the good Marshal's hat might be lulled into a false sense of security and land on his own head by mistake. Pommes Frites didn't have a very high opinion of pigeons and although he had never actually caught one, he refused to discount the possibility.

Rotating himself as far as was practicable while standing on three legs, he watched the object pass overhead. Ignoring any possibilities the Café l'Esplanade on the corner of the *Place* might have in the way of refreshment, oblivious to the landing facilities offered up by the Esplanade des Invalides below and to its right, the object gained height again and with gathering speed disappeared over the top of some nearby buildings just as Monsieur Pamplemousse came up out of the Metro.

Much to Pommes Frites' disappointment, his master barely gave it a second glance. He, too, had other, more important things on his mind. Having registered the object, he dismissed it as a mere toy; the temporary plaything of some spoilt brat who lived in the nearby sixteenth and whose parents had more money than sense. Only the week before he'd seen a miniature tank in one of the department stores on the Boulevard Haussmann. The price had been more than the cost of his own car.

The possibility that its presence might have anything to do with his being summoned at an unusually early hour for a meeting with the Director didn't cross his mind.

Monsieur Pamplemousse mistrusted such summonses – especially when they happened to come during the middle of breakfast, and even more so when by rights he should be enjoying a well-earned week off from his travels. Doucette had not been best pleased at the news. He had promised to take her shopping that morning for some new curtain material. There had been much banging of crockery in the kitchen and he'd had to exercise care with his *croissant* lest too many crumbs found their way onto the floor. It had not been a good start to the day.

As they took advantage of a gap in the traffic and crossed the road a feeling of gloom set in. Even the all-pervading smell of fresh lime from the trees surrounding the Esplanade, normally sufficient to put him in a good humour whatever the circumstances, failed to have its usual effect. The thought he had been entertaining of telephoning Doucette when he reached the office – just to see how she was getting on – no longer seemed such a good idea. She would start asking questions about what time she could expect him back and would he want lunch and if so, what? He would become irritated because he would have no idea of the answer.

He paused at the corner of the *Place*, wondering whether he should stop by at the *café* for a quick *eau-de-vie* – a little 'Dutch courage'. If he was honest he had another reason besides shopping for not wanting to go into the office that morning. Madame Grante was on the warpath, and when Madame Grante was on the warpath, 'retreat' was the only sensible course. Sniping was prevalent and mortar fire unremitting in its intensity.

The current hostilities had to do with his last assignment for *Le Guide*, an assignment which had not been of his making, and which through no fault of his own had involved him in expenditure over and above that normally agreed to in staff regulations. Expenditure of a kind which, when detailed in black and white on a P39, made Madame Grante's lips – which could never by any stretch of the imagination be described as full, let alone generous – become so compressed it was hard to tell where the bottom one finished and the top one began, except when they parted company in order to permit the escape of some freshly barbed comment. Things had reached such a pass that instead of eating in the canteen he had taken to having sandwiches sent up to his room rather than run the risk of bumping into her in a corridor, knowing full well that she was probably lying in wait for him.

He could hear her voice now as she reeled off the list from his claim sheet, savouring each and every word in tones which would not have disgraced a leading member of the *Comédie Française* reciting her favourite piece to the back row of the *fauteuils*.

'Braided nylon fishing thread, fifty metres. One cylinder of gas, helium, large. Photographic chemicals, various. Inflatable dog kennel, one. Twenty-two pairs of ladies' *culottes*, black . . .'

It was the unfairness of it all that particularly grieved Monsieur Pamplemousse. His expenses sheet should never have arrived on Madame Grante's desk in the first place, and wouldn't have done so had it not been for a clerical error somewhere along the line. It had been intended for the eyes of certain unnamed people in a department of the Ministry of the Interior. Promises had been made. Secrecy had been the order of the day.

In the end he had gone to the Director and asked him to put

his foot down. Very reluctantly the Director had agreed.

There the matter should have ended, and in the normal course of events would have done, had it not been for the fact that it wasn't in Madame Grante's nature to let any matter rest until she was in full possession of the facts. The silence following her brief interview on the top floor didn't, in Monsieur Pamplemousse's view, mean that all was forgotten, still less forgiven.

Taking a card from an inside pocket, he paused outside an anonymous building a little way along the Rue Fabert and held it against a plate in the wall alongside a pair of wooden doors. There was an answering buzz and a smaller door set into one of the larger ones swung open. Closing it behind them he led the way across a paved courtyard and round the fountain in the centre. Noting the Director's Citroën CX25 was already in its privileged parking space he automatically glanced towards the top floor. He was just in time to see the Director himself disappearing around a corner of the balcony outside his office. He appeared to be in a hurry and he was carrying some kind of walkie-talkie, or possibly a radio-telephone. For despite *Le Guide*'s deep-rooted sense of tradition and resistance to change, he prided himself on keeping abreast of the latest developments. The operations room in the basement would not have looked out of place in the Headquarters of NATO or even a James Bond movie.

While awaiting his arrival, the Director had no doubt been enjoying the morning sunshine while indulging in his favourite pastime of counting the 'Stock Pots' of Paris. His suite of offices was a recent addition to the main offices, occupying the whole of a mansard floor which lifted it above the rooftops of the surrounding buildings. Like the bridge of a great ocean liner, it afforded an unrivalled view of everything that went on below, and from the balcony which encircled it the Director, in his role of Captain, was able to keep a weather eye on the world outside. On special occasions – such as Bastille Day – he often held parties when he treated his guests to a guided tour of those restaurants in Paris fortunate enough to be awarded a 'Stock Pot' in *Le Guide* for their culinary achievements. It was his proud boast that on a clear day it was possible with the aid of a pair of binoculars to pick out a grand total of over one hundred such establishments, no less than four of which bore the supreme accolade of three 'Stock Pots', thereby being accorded the honour of having their exact position pin-pointed by means of a brass plate engraved with an arrow let into the stone balustrade.

Monsieur Pamplemousse was about to go on his way when he stopped dead in his tracks, his eyes riveted by the spectacle above him. The object which only a few minutes before he'd seen floating above the *Place* suddenly came into view again above their heads. For a moment or two it hovered in what appeared to be an agony of indecision, and then, just as the Director came rushing back around the corner still clutching his device, it disappeared through an open door and into his office.

All in all, Monsieur Pamplemousse wasn't sorry he'd resisted the temptation to stop for a drink on the way in. At least he knew he had seen what he had seen while stone cold sober.

Pommes Frites suffered no such inhibitions. Fearing the worst as he followed his master through the revolving door of the main building, he let out another warning howl.

But Monsieur Pamplemousse's feeling of virtue was short-lived. Almost immediately he changed his mind – an *eau-de-vie* would have gone down very well indeed at that moment. Standing by the reception desk, a sheaf of papers clutched in her right hand, was Madame Grante. She was talking to the receptionist. That she had been lying in wait was patently obvious, for no sooner were they through the door than she came forward to greet them. He braced himself for the onslaught, while Pommes Frites, ever sensitive to his master's moods, almost imperceptibly but nonetheless firmly, bared his teeth.

However, both were guilty of over-reacting. For once, Madame Grante seemed all sweetness and light.

Her '*Bonjour*, Monsieur Pamplemousse!' was trilled in such spring-like tones, and the accompanying smile was so sunny, that even Pommes Frites had the grace to look ashamed when she turned it in his direction.

'*Bonjour*, Madame Grante.' Much to Monsieur Pamplemousse's annoyance, his voice came out higher than he'd intended. He cleared his throat, wondering what to say next, but fortunately he was saved by the ping of a lift bell.

Once inside the safety of the lift he pressed the button for the top floor as quickly as possible in case she decided to follow them in.

As the doors slid shut he pondered both the Director's strange behaviour and that of Madame Grante, wondering if the two were linked in any way. Madame Grante on the warpath was one thing; at least you knew where you were. The new Madame Grante was something else again, and he wasn't quite sure how to cope with it. Had he detected another element in her welcoming smile? A gleam of triumph, perhaps? No, it had been something else. Something he couldn't quite put his finger on. Anticipation? Whatever it was he had a nasty feeling in the back of his mind that it spelt trouble. He would need to watch himself.

Exchanging greetings with the Director's secretary in the outer office, he crossed the room and knocked on the inner door.

To his surprise, it was opened almost immediately.

'Aristide, *entrez, entrez*. And Pommes Frites. *Comment allez-vous?*'

The Director bent down to give Pommes Frites a welcoming pat and then hastily withdrew his hand as the object of his attentions bristled. It was all too apparent that flattery would be a waste of time. Pommes Frites' attentions were concentrated elsewhere.

Monsieur Pamplemousse was about to remonstrate when he, too, stiffened. There, in the centre of the Director's desk, stood a model airship. Seen at close quarters, it was not unlike the tiny replicas of aircraft one saw in the office windows of the great airlines in the Avenue des Champs Elysées, albeit, since he had seen it flying with his own eyes, much more sophisticated. Obviously the work of a master craftsman, for it was complete in every detail, even down to replicas of passengers and crew who could be seen through the Perspex windows in the side, it was attached to a small mooring tower underneath which lay an open map of Europe.

The Director beamed as he followed the direction of their gaze. Crossing to his desk, he gazed reverently at the object. 'What do you think of it, Aristide?'

For a second time in as many minutes, Monsieur Pamplemousse found himself at a loss for words.

'It is a birthday present for your nephew, *Monsieur*? I'm sure he will be delighted.'

The Director made a clucking noise. 'No, Pamplemousse, it is not a birthday present for my nephew.'

Rather than risk further displeasure, Monsieur Pamplemousse decided not to essay another reply to the question, but in the event it was followed almost immediately by a second.

'Picture this dirigible inflated to several thousand times its present size,' continued the Director. 'What would you see?'

Suspecting a trick question, Monsieur Pamplemousse took his time. 'I see a lot of small pieces, *Monsieur*,' he said innocently. 'Surely it would explode?'

The Director gazed at him in silence. He had the look on his face of a man wondering whether or not he had made the right decision over some important matter. His lips moved, but nothing came out. Eventually, after what seemed like an eternity, he waved Pamplemousse towards the armchair opposite his desk and began pacing the room while gathering his thoughts.

'No doubt,' he said at last, 'you have read in the *journaux* about the inauguration of a new airship service between Brittany and *Grande-Bretagne*?'

Monsieur Pamplemousse nodded. 'I have seen pictures of it, *Monsieur*.' The newspapers had been full of them lately.

14

'Good.' The Director looked better pleased. 'It is an out-ward manifestation of the *entente cordiale* agreement signed in 1904, the reaffirmation of which our respective Govern-ments have been working towards in recent months. It is only a small step, especially when compared with the tunnel which is at this very moment being constructed beneath *La Manche* to link our two countries by rail, but an important one nevertheless.

'The dirigible, Pamplemousse, is the transportation of the future; an elegant solution to powered flight. Word has gone out from the Elysée Palace itself that it must not fail. We are entering a new era of graciousness. It combines the best of the old with that of the new; on the one hand embracing all that we have grown up with and love and cherish, whilst at the same time reaching out towards new frontiers. Above all, it is safe. The hazardous days of the old *Graf Zeppelin* have gone forever.'

Monsieur Pamplemousse remained silent. It was hard to see where the Director's flights of rhetoric were leading him. Romantic though the possibility might be of transporting up to a dozen people in comparative luxury, it hardly compared with a direct rail link in terms of either numbers or value for money. Clearly there was more to come.

'Besides which,' continued the Director, 'it will help quieten the vociferous minority who feel Brittany is neglected and would dearly like to see it become a separate state. With an election on the horizon that is not unimportant. No doubt the scheme appeals to the British government because they will be manufacturing the dirigibles. If successful, it could well be the first of many.

'Be that as it may, both governments have their own reasons for attaching great importance to the affair. So much so that the respective heads of state have agreed to take part in the inaugural flight four days from now.'

The Director paused by his desk and then lowered his voice. 'All I have told you so far, Pamplemousse, is common knowledge. I come now to my reason for asking you here at

15

such short notice. We are at present in a crisis situation.'

Carefully moving the airship and its mooring tower to one side, he picked up the map. 'The inaugural flight commences at eleven hundred hours on Friday. The dirigible will take off from a small airfield north of La Baule and will touch down just over six hours later on a similar landing strip south of London – a distance of some five hundred kilometres. What, Pamplemousse, will those aboard be most in need of during the time they are aloft? I ask, because even though I have repeated the same question to myself countless times, I still cannot believe no one thought of it.'

'You mean . . . there are no facilities on board?' Monsieur Pamplemousse looked suitably staggered. 'That is indeed a grave oversight.'

'No, Pamplemousse, that is not what I mean. In the current situation "facilities" of the kind you doubtless have in mind are low on the agenda.'

'But *Monsieur*, with respect, six hours is a long time. After all that food and drink . . .'

'As things stand at the moment, Pamplemousse, there will be no food and drink. There will be no food and drink for the very simple reason that no one has thought to provide any. For weeks people have been planning. Schedules have been drawn up, security arrangements tested. Everything that could possibly go wrong has been thought of. Every aspect of the programme has been covered, not once but time and time again. All except the one vital factor, sustenance.'

The Director paused to let his words sink in before resuming.

'Imagine the atmosphere aloft if thirteen hundred hours came and went and there was no sign of *déjeuner*. It would be icy in the extreme. *Entente* would be far from *cordiale*. Had the arrangements been made in *Angleterre* one might have understood. They would probably have been happy to make do with sandwiches and a thermos of hot tea – although to give them their due, even that would be better than nothing – but for *La Belle France* to make such a cardinal error – poof!

16

It is hard to credit. We shall be the laughing-stock of Europe. Heads will roll, of course, but that doesn't solve the immediate problem. Which is where, Aristide, we come in. Or rather, *you* do.'

'I, *Monsieur*?' Monsieur Pamplemousse sat bolt upright. Had the Director suddenly let off a shotgun at close range he could hardly have been more startled.

The Director assumed his 'all has been decided, yours is not to reason why' tones. '*Le Guide* has been charged with making good the omission. We have been given *carte blanche*. Of course, Michelin will be piqued and Gault–Millau will be seething. Both will probably take umbrage, but that cannot be helped. If all goes well it will be a considerable *plume* in our *chapeau*.'

The interior of a cupboard became illuminated as he opened it to reach inside for a bottle of champagne. 'I think this calls for a celebration, although I must admit the whole thing came about by sheer chance.

'It so happened that last night I was dining with a group of friends, some of whom are highly placed, and the subject of the conversation turned to that of the dirigible.

'Purely out of professional interest I enquired as to the nature of the catering arrangements. Aristide, you could have sliced the silence which followed my remark with a *couteau à beurre*.

'I won't bore you with all that followed. Someone, whose name I cannot disclose, left the table to make a telephone call. When he returned, looking, I may say, a trifle pale, names were bandied around. One by one they were abandoned. Bocuse is in Japan on one of his tours. Vergé is in America. We went through the list, and to cut a long story short, suddenly they all turned and looked in my direction.'

The cork was removed with the discreetest of pops and the Director held up two glasses to the light to check their cleanliness before pouring. 'The honour of France is in your hands, Aristide. I need hardly say that not a word of this must be breathed to anyone. That is one of the main reasons why you have been selected. Your vast experience in matters of security coupled with your extraordinary palate and your natural sense of discretion make you an ideal choice.

'I can think of no better person for the job, Pample-mousse.' The Director raised his glass. 'Your very good health, and here's to the success of your mission. I have already drawn up some preliminary notes for a possible menu, but naturally I leave the final choice to you.'

Monsieur Pamplemousse sipped his champagne reflec-tively. It was his favourite – Gosset. He judged it to be a '62. There was a distinct flavour of hazelnuts. The Director must have got it in specially. All part of the softening up process, no doubt. Not that it was necessary; the whole idea sounded intriguing. He would willingly postpone his holiday. This would be a challenge.

'You say the airfield is north of La Baule, *Monsieur*?'

'It is just outside a little place called Port St. Augustin. You may know it. An ideal location for those wishing to arrive in style at what is probably the best beach in Europe.'

Port St. Augustin. Monsieur Pamplemousse remembered it well, although it was many years since he'd last been in the area.

'Madame Pamplemousse and I went there soon after we got married, *Monsieur*. We stayed at the Hôtel du Port. It is perched on the rocks overlooking the harbour . . .'

'Ah, yes.' The Director looked less than enthusiastic. 'The Hôtel du Port is full, I'm afraid.'

'There was one other. The Hôtel du Centre, I believe it was called.'

'That too, is fully booked.' For some reason Monsieur Pamplemousse thought he detected a note of unease creeping into the other's voice. 'It is always the same in Brittany. The season is short and the same people go there year after year.

'However, a reservation has been made for you from tomorrow evening onwards at a small hotel just outside the village – the Ty Coz. I am told some of the rooms have a view of the sea, although the view inland is said to be equally good.

18

The choice is yours.'

Monsieur Pamplemousse was tempted to ask why, if everywhere else was so crowded, he could get into the Ty Coz with a choice of rooms, but the Director was in full flight.

'The Hôtel has been recommended to me in the strongest possible terms. It seems the owner has invented a whole new cuisine, *La Cuisine Régionale Naturelle*. And in southern Brittany, Aristide, we all know what that means. Luscious lobsters, fresh from their pots. Tunny fish from Concarneau, sardines from La Turballe, mussels and oysters from the Morbihan . . . It will be an ideal opportunity to carry out an investigation.

'Ah, Aristide,' the Director crossed to his desk and gazed lovingly at the airship. 'All that and a ride in a dirigible to boot. I wish I could come too, but alas, I am on a diet.'

He picked up the small black object which Monsieur Pamplemousse had seen him holding in his hand earlier, and which he now realised was a radio-control module. 'Would you care for a go, Aristide?'

'May I, *Monsieur*?'

The Director detached the airship carefully from its mooring and gathered it tenderly in his arms. 'If you don't mind, I will carry out the initial launch. It is the only model in existence and it wouldn't do to have an accident. Once it is airborne you will soon get the feel of the controls.'

Monsieur Pamplemousse followed him out onto the balcony and watched while adjustments were being made and the twin motors set in motion.

'It is a complete replica in every detail.' Like a small boy with a new toy, the Director could hardly keep the excitement from his voice as he licked his finger and held it up to test the wind direction. 'As I said earlier, no expense has been spared to ensure the success of the enterprise; no stone left unturned . . .'

'Except one,' Monsieur Pamplemousse found the Director's enthusiasm infectious.

19

'Indeed, Aristide. Except one. The reason for my being given the loan of this is so that we can see for ourselves the ergonomics of the task ahead. Is there, *par exemple*, room for a dessert chariot, and if so, how large?' Shading his eyes against the sun, the Director released his hold on the craft and then watched as it set off, uncertainly at first, and then with rapidly gathering speed in the direction of the wide open space of the Esplanade des Invalides.

'You may take over now, Pamplemousse.'

Feeling slightly nervous now that the actual moment had arrived, Monsieur Pamplemousse took the control unit and began tentatively moving an array of levers.

On the square below an *autobus* was disgorging a load of Japanese tourists, all of whom were so busy rushing to and fro taking photographs of each other in groups of varying size and complexity they quite failed to see what was going on above their heads. Monsieur Pamplemousse reflected that had they but known, they were missing a golden opportunity to surprise and delight their friends back home.

He suddenly realised he'd been concentrating so hard he hadn't noticed the Director was talking again.

'I was saying, Pamplemousse, I should try and avoid flying too close to the Hôtel des Invalides. It wouldn't do to attract the attention of the guards. One of them might draw his revolver and attempt to shoot it down. I have promised to return it safely by this afternoon at the latest. The President himself has yet to see it. No doubt he will wish to have a go inside the Palace grounds.'

'*Oui, Monsieur.*' Monsieur Pamplemousse moved a lever to the left and watched as the airship began executing a turn to port. It really was most enjoyable. Perhaps when he got back from Brittany he would investigate some more modest version of the toy. A radio-controlled boat, perhaps? The possibilities were endless.

As he moved another control and set the craft into a downward path which would bring it level with the top of the balcony he felt a stirring behind him. It heralded the arrival of

Pommes Frites on the scene.

Pommes Frites blinked as he emerged from the Director's office onto the sunlit balcony. Having enjoyed a short nap while the others were talking, he'd woken to find he was alone and that the voices were now coming from outside. Something was going on, and feeling left out of things he decided – quite reasonably in his view – to find out what it was.

He arrived just as his master was about to carry out the delicate manoeuvre of making the final approach; a manoeuvre which would have been difficult enough at the best of times, but made more so by a sudden downward draught of cold air created by the temperature of the water issuing from the fountain in the courtyard below. It was a manoeuvre which needed the utmost concentration and which most certainly would have been brought to a more successful conclusion, had not what felt like a ton weight suddenly landed on his shoulders just at the *moment critique*.

Catching sight of Pommes Frites, and anticipating his next move, the Director issued a warning cry, but it was too late. Watched by all three, the dirigible lost height rapidly and disappeared at speed through an open window several floors below.

A feeling of gloom descended on the balcony. It was as though a large black cloud had suddenly obscured the sun.

'Let us hope,' said the Director, 'that Madame Grante manages to shut off the motors before too much damage is done. I think it was her window the dirigible entered. I trust, also, that it is not an omen.'

Without bothering to reply, Monsieur Pamplemousse bounded through the Director's office, past an astonished secretary, and out into the corridor. Eschewing the lift, and with Pommes Frites hard on his heels, he shot down three floors, arriving outside Madame Grante's office without even bothering to draw breath. There was a possibility, a very faint possibility, that she would be out of her room.

But as he opened the door he came to an abrupt halt.

Patently the room was far from empty. There were papers everywhere. It looked as though it had been struck by a minor hurricane.

Madame Grante was in the act of closing the door of her stationery cupboard on the far side of the room.

She turned. 'Monsieur Pamplemousse?'

'Madame Grante.' He took a deep breath and pulled himself together. 'Madame Grante, I was wondering . . . that is to say . . . may we have our balloon back, *s'il vous plaît?*'

With a flourish Madame Grante deposited a silver key in a place where it would have needed a braver man than Monsieur Pamplemousse to retrieve it. 'Your balloon, Monsieur Pamplemousse? I see no balloon.'

For a full thirty seconds they stood staring at each other. Once again he was conscious of a look in Madame Grante's eyes he couldn't quite make out. It was something more than mere triumph.

Wild thoughts of declaring his undying love for her crossed his mind and were instantly dismissed. Bernard always said you never could tell; still waters ran deep. But Bernard had theories about most things. The prospect of Madame Grante melting in his arms was not only remote, it didn't bear thinking about. Such a declaration might even send her into a state of shock. Not to mention the possible effect on Pommes Frites. Would it get him what he wanted? More important still, would it be worth it?

For the sake of the Director? Certainly not!

For the sake of France? No, not even for that!

Monsieur Pamplemousse knew when he was beaten. He turned on his heels and left, making his way up to the top floor at a somewhat slower rate than he had come down.

The Director was waiting outside his door. His face fell as Monsieur Pamplemousse came into view. 'You are empty-handed. Don't tell me . . .'

Monsieur Pamplemousse nodded. 'I am afraid we are in trouble, *Monsieur*. Madame Grante has put the dirigible where she keeps her P39s.'

'And the key, Pamplemousse? Where is the key?'

'The key, *Monsieur*, is in a place which is even more impregnable than her store cupboard. It is where she keeps her *doudounes*!'

The Director clutched at the door frame for support. 'This bodes ill, Pamplemousse!' he exclaimed. 'I am not by nature a superstitious man, but I fear this bodes ill for us all.'

2

A Surfeit of Nuns

Monsieur Pamplemousse focused his Leica camera on the off side of his 2CV, or the little of it which could still be seen above the top of a ditch, and operated the shutter several times. As he did so he pondered, not for the first time in his life, on the immutability of the laws of fate which decreed that following a series of seemingly unconnected events one should, for better or worse, find oneself at a certain spot at a certain time, not a second before nor a split-second after that moment which had all the appearances of being pre-ordained.

His present situation definitely came under the second category. If fate had indeed had a hand in things then someone, somewhere on high, had it in for him. His star was not in the ascendant.

He shivered a little, partly from delayed shock and partly from the cool breeze which was blowing in from the sea. He licked his lips. They tasted of salt. Glancing up he registered the fact that the same breeze was bringing with it a bank of dark rain clouds and he hoped it was only a passing storm. The sky to the west still looked bright enough and the long-term forecast was good, but even a minor shower would be bad news in the circumstances. Short of getting back in the car – which wouldn't be easy – shelter was non-existent. Pommes Frites would be all right. At least he had his inflatable kennel, but there certainly wouldn't be room in it for both of them.

If only he hadn't decided on the spur of the moment to branch off the D99 at Guérande. It hadn't even been a short cut; a voyage of remembrance rather than one of discovery, an exercise in nostalgia. If he'd stuck to the main road he would have been in Port St. Augustin by now, sampling the delights of *La Cuisine Régionale Naturelle*.

Long before that there had been lunch.

Not that he regretted his meal, but it had been a far more protracted affair than he'd intended. One of his colleagues, Glandier, had left a note in his tray back at the office concerning a little restaurant he'd come across on the bank of one of the Loire's many tributaries. Any recommendation from Glandier was worth following up, and on the strength of it he'd made a detour.

In the event it had exceeded all his expectations. Over a Kir made with ice-cold *aligoté* and served at a little table under a tree by the river, he had been able to watch the work going on in the kitchen, while making the first of many notes to come during the meal.

The first course – a cucumber salad – had been exactly right. Peeled, split down the middle, its seeds removed, the cucumber had been cut paper thin and sprinkled with salt to draw out all the excess liquid, leaving it, after draining, limp, yet deliciously crunchy. The vinegar and oil in the dressing had been of good quality with just the right amount of sugar added to counteract the natural bitterness. But it was the addition of the few freshwater crayfish which had lifted the dish above the norm.

With a basketful of crisp, fresh bread and a glass or two of sparkling Vouvray to help it down, he'd been of a mind to call it a day; a refreshing break in an otherwise long and tedious journey. But then he'd caught sight of some trout being brought to the back door of the restaurant by someone he had earlier seen fishing further along the river bank and the temptation to explore the menu still further had proved too great to resist.

It had been a wise decision.

Coated in oil and rolled in flour before being seared in hot butter – quickly enough so that it didn't stick to the pan, but not so hot that the flour formed a crust – the fish had arrived at the table golden brown. A little lemon juice and some fresh blanched parsley had been added to the butter in which the trout had been cooked and made a golden foam as it was poured over the top at the last moment. The *pommes frites* were as perfect an accompaniment as one could wish for.

But it was the dessert which was undoubtedly the *pièce de résistance*. When Monsieur Pamplemousse saw a man at a nearby table – obviously a regular – tucking into a jam omelette with such gusto and dabbing of the lips with his napkin that it was like a cabaret act, he'd quickly succumbed.

As with the trout, the omelette arrived at his table at exactly the right moment. Piping hot, the icing-sugar on the top caramelised in a criss-cross pattern by the use of a red-hot metal skewer, the *confiture* inside of a quality which indicated it had never seen the inside of a shop let alone a factory. He could still taste it.

Even Pommes Frites, not normally a jam-eater, had signalled his approval, which was praise indeed. The look on his face as his master slipped him a portion said it all. Even so, with a long journey ahead of them, to have indulged in a second helping had been folly of the very worst kind. A feeling of somnolence had set in uncomfortably soon after they set off on the last part of their journey. Snores had started to issue from the back of the *Deux Chevaux* long before they reached the N23.

Driving along, Monsieur Pamplemousse had fallen to thinking about his work, and that, too, had slowed him down. Deep inside there was the usual conflict which began when he came across somewhere new, a battle between the desire to share his pleasures and a selfish wish to keep them to himself. He had no doubt that Glandier felt the same way too. All too frequently, discovery and a mention in *Le Guide* brought success, but with success came different pressures and often changes for the worse. It would be sad to come back another year and find the tranquil field at the side of the hotel turned into a car park smelling of petrol fumes, disturbing the peace and quiet of this lovely backwater with the sound of revving engines and slamming doors. But you couldn't have it both ways.

He gave a sigh as he regarded his 2CV. He couldn't have it both ways either. Normally he prided himself on his reactions at the wheel, but they had been dulled by over-eating; over-eating and, he had to admit, perhaps one glass of wine too many?

On the other hand, who would have expected to encounter in an area such as the *Marais Salant* – a vast unrelieved mosaic of grey salt pans, flat as a pancake as far as the eye could see – a car travelling on the wrong side of the road. He felt very aggrieved. It wasn't as though it had been driven by some maniac English tourist admiring the view – there would have been some excuse then; it had been full of nuns. Nuns who had so far forgotten the basic tenets of their calling that they hadn't even bothered to stop to make sure he was unharmed. For all they knew he might have needed the last rites. That they had seen him drive into the ditch he hadn't the slightest doubt; at the very last moment he'd caught a glimpse of two white faces peering out at him from the rear window of the car as it disappeared in a cloud of dust.

He wondered what the world was coming to. A few well-chosen words in the ear of the Mother Superior would not come amiss, but he'd been so taken aback by the whole incident he'd failed to register the number of the car – an old Peugeot 404. Given his background and training that was unforgivable. He must be getting old.

The really galling thing about the whole affair was that he'd seen the car coming towards him long before it arrived, starting as a tiny speck on the horizon and growing in size until it had loomed inescapably large as they met on the corner, forcing him to take evasive action at the last possible moment by driving into the ditch.

Fortunately no great damage had been done, and apart from looking somewhat dazed, Pommes Frites was in one piece. The far side of the ditch was higher than the other, being part of a long platform on which salt was piled to dry off in the sun, and the grass which covered the sides had acted as a cushion. But the possibility of getting his car back onto the road again all by himself was remote. He made a few desultory attempts, but one rear wheel was lifted clear off the ground and even with Pommes Frites' weight on the back seat, that was where it stayed. He would need the help of a tractor, and looking around the area, mechanical aids of any sort seemed to have low priority in ensuring the continuing supplies of sea salt to the tables of France.

Bleak was perhaps the best way of describing the country-side; bleak, but with a strange, almost translucent light. In the distance across the empty landscape he could see the occasional figure of someone working late, but they were all too far away to notice his plight, or to do much about it if they did.

A sandpiper flew past.

Four cars came and went, but they were all going the wrong way and full of holidaymakers. He glanced at his watch. It was just after six-thirty. They were probably the last he would see for a while. Most visitors would be back in their hotels by now, getting ready for the evening meal, having left the beach early because of the approaching clouds. After a long day on the sea-front those with families were probably glad of the excuse.

Just as the first rain began to fall he saw a car coming towards him, travelling the way he wanted to go. It was being driven fast, and as it drew near he saw there was a girl at the wheel.

Signalling Pommes Frites to stay where he was, Monsieur Pamplemousse decided to abandon his own car and leapt into the road, waving his arms. Almost immediately, he jumped back again, nearly losing his balance as the black BMW shot past, swerved, then skidded to a halt a little way along the road. He might have been killed. Regardless of the rights and wrongs of stopping for strangers, there were ways of going about it. For a moment he almost regretted no longer being in the Force. In the old days he'd thrown the book at drivers for less.

There was a roar from the engine and a moment later the car reversed towards him. At least the girl wasn't leaving him to his fate like the others. It skidded to a halt and he waited impatiently for the electrically operated window to be lowered.

Sizing up the situation with a quick glance the girl reached over and released the door catch. 'You'll get soaked. You'd better get in.'

'I have a companion.' Monsieur Pamplemousse pointed to Pommes Frites. 'And some *bagages*. I'm afraid we have had an accident. Some *imbéciles* nuns driving on the wrong side of the road. If you would be so kind . . .'

There was only a moment's hesitation. 'He'd better get in the back. I'll look after him. You see to the rest. The compartment is unlocked.'

Pommes Frites was in the back of the car almost before his master had time to get their luggage out, watching proceedings through the rain-spattered glass, making sure his own things were safely installed.

The boot was empty save for a small and expensive-looking valise and a roll of coarse material which he had to move before he could get his own belongings in. There was also a strong smell of pear-drops.

Monsieur Pamplemousse closed the boot and ran round the side of the car, reaching for his handkerchief as he went. He could feel the water running down his face in tiny rivulets.

'It is very kind of you.' He climbed in, mopping his brow. In the circumstances gratitude was very much in order. He could hardly complain that a moment or too earlier she had nearly run him down. 'I'm sorry if we have delayed you.'

The implication that she'd been going too fast was not lost.

'I hope I didn't frighten you too much. I was reaching for the lights as I came round the corner and your car was hidden from view. Besides, I didn't expect you to jump out from nowhere. What happened?'

'We are on our way to Port St. Augustin. We were making a detour as it happened . . .'

'Port St. Augustin! But that is where I am going. I can take you all the way. Where are you staying?'

'The Ty Coz.'

'I do not know the name. I know only the Hôtel du Port, but we can look for it. The town is not large.'

As he settled back in his seat, Monsieur Pamplemousse suddenly felt warm and comfortable and at peace with the world. Out of the corner of his eye he could see that Pommes Frites felt the same way too. Dog-like, he had already assumed the proprietorial air of an owner-driver, gazing out of the window at the passing scene as if he did it every day of his life. Perhaps it was their presence in the car, not the accident leading up to it, that had been pre-ordained by the giant computer in the sky. Now there was a thought.

He stole a sideways glance at the girl. Obviously she was not a local. He doubted if she was even French. Although she spoke the language well, she sounded foreign. Italian, perhaps. Or Greek. She had a dark, olive-skinned complexion which suggested the southern Mediterranean. She was gypsy-like. Her hair was long and jet-black. In a few years it would probably be too long, but time was still on her side. Her skin was smooth and unwrinkled. She drove quickly and with precision, taking advantage of every bend and camber in the road. He felt safe with her and changed his mind about the 'incident'. Perhaps, he told himself, he had been at fault for not giving her more warning.

By now they were almost out of the marshes and the giant sardine canneries of La Turballe loomed into view. They were preceded by a row of modern-looking shops and flats. He wondered about getting out there and then in the hope of finding a garage, but the first one they saw was already

30

closed. He gave up the idea. He had no wish to be stranded with all his luggage.

Almost as quickly as it had begun, the rain stopped. Out to sea the sun was shining. Any moment now it would be shining on them too. He found himself looking for the inevitable rainbow. Keeping her eyes on the traffic ahead, which was beginning to build up, the girl switched off the wipers and leaned across to adjust the demister. Her hands looked strong, almost masculine, and yet well cared for – the nails short and business-like. If she wore any perfume it didn't register, and yet there was a curious, indefinable scent of something which stirred memories in the back of his mind. Make-up was minimal. With her looks it would have been an unnecessary embellishment.

He allowed himself a longer look while her attention was otherwise engaged.

She was wearing a loose-fitting jump suit. Dark green, the colour of her eyes. She might have been a garage mechanic for all it did for her figure, but as she leaned forward he was very conscious that what was underneath was the whole person and nothing but the person. Only someone confident enough to know the effect that would have could have got away with wearing it. Or perhaps she didn't care.

'Well, do I pass?'

He came down to earth with a jerk. 'I'm sorry. To be truthful, it is very rude of me, I know . . . but I was wondering what you do for a living.'

'And?'

'You don't look as though you are on holiday and you are not a housewife. At least, you do not drive like one.'

'You can tell a housewife by the way she drives?' She was mocking him, and yet it was done with good humour.

'Not exactly. But it is a process of elimination.' He felt he might be on dangerous ground. 'Housewives who own a BMW 325i are in the minority. If it is their husband's car, then they usually drive with care – they are frightened of scratching it.'

'Being married doesn't necessarily turn you into a house-wife, nor does it stop you doing something you enjoy doing well.'

Outside La Turballe they met a long line of traffic. She overtook two cars quickly and easily, then slipped into a gap behind a third.

'You are also good at making decisions.'

'Housewives do not make decisions?' Again it was said with a half smile.

'Constantly. Thousands every day. But on the whole they are minor ones. They are not usually a matter of life and death . . .'

He broke off, allowing her to concentrate as she pulled out to overtake the car in front. They passed a rose-filled garden, then hedgerows with occasional patches of yellow gorse. The countryside was in full bloom. He could see giant clover and daisies everywhere. Fields of camomile bordered the road.

'That is very perspicacious of you.' She laughed. 'You will never guess.'

It was a challenge he found hard to resist. Suddenly, it was like playing a television game. It gave him the freedom to make wild statements. He almost asked to see her 'mime'.

'If I found myself in a tight corner I wouldn't mind having you beside me and I wouldn't worry about you as I might about others.'

'What a strange thing to say. Are you often in a tight corner?'

'Occasionally. I used to be at one time.'

It was her turn to look intrigued. She stole a quick side-ways glance as they dropped in behind another lorry.

'Tell me more.'

He avoided the question. 'I couldn't help noticing your hands just now. They are well cared for, and yet they are also very strong. You also, if I may say so, have an extremely good figure. For what you do you must keep very fit, or vice versa.'

'That is true.'

32

'Fit and strong, so you must do it regularly.'

'That is also true.'

'And you are happy in your work?'

She hesitated for a fraction of a second. 'Very. It is my life. I am lucky. To be fit and well and to have work that also makes you happy is a great blessing. I couldn't wish for more.'

That, thought Monsieur Pamplemousse, is not the total and absolute truth. There are other things you wish for. He wondered what they were.

'And you? Are you happy in *your* work?'

'Very.' A quarter of an hour before he wouldn't have said that. A quarter of an hour ago, standing in the rain beside his overturned car, he had been far from happy. 'I couldn't wish for more either.'

'I think perhaps you enjoy food. There is a fresh stain on your tie, and you have – please forgive me . . .' for the first time she sounded embarrassed, unsure of herself. 'You have been eating garlic recently.'

He was about to deny it. Nothing he'd eaten for *déjeuner* had contained a scrap of garlic. Then he remembered that Doucette had given him a plate of *saucisson* for breakfast on account of the journey. Between them, he and Pommes Frites had eaten the lot.

She was one up. 'Yes, I do like food. That is *my* life.'

'And that puts you in danger?'

Before he had time to answer, a signpost for Port St. Augustin came into view. She flicked the indicator and pulled over to the left to enter an intersection. They waited for traffic coming the other way to pass.

'Sometimes. It is a throwback from my previous work. If it is true that some people tend to attract problems, then I tend to attract "situations". Or perhaps I look for them.' He rarely brought it into conversation, preferring to remain anonymous, and he wasn't entirely sure why he was saying it now. 'For many years I was with the Paris *Sûreté*.'

She clicked her fingers. 'Of course, I knew I had seen you

33

somewhere before. Or rather, not you, your picture. You have an unusual name.'

'Pamplemousse. I was sometimes in the *journaux*.' That was an understatement. There had been a time when, for one reason or another, it felt as though he was never out of them. Once, after being involved in a notorious case which had hit the headlines, he'd even had a feature article written about him in *Paris Match*. It had pursued him for years.

Seeing a gap in the traffic, she glanced quickly in both directions before accelerating off the main road.

He was suddenly conscious of a change in the atmosphere. It was as though a shutter had come down. She seemed nervous and kept looking in the mirror. He wondered if she had noticed something. On the pretext of seeing how Pommes Frites was getting on he turned round in his seat and took a quick look out of the back window. A dark blue van was just turning off the main road. It was too far away to identify, but the girl evidently saw it too, for he felt her accelerate and they took the next corner at a speed which startled him.

Unobtrusively, he slid his hand down and tightened his safety belt. But he needn't have worried. His companion was much too busy with her own thoughts to notice. The earthy, almost animal-like quality he had noticed earlier was now even more apparent. She was like a deer on the run. Tense, alert . . .

'*Alors!*' As they reached the outskirts of Port St. Augustin he glimpsed a row of posters and the penny dropped.

'You are with a circus!'

She nodded. He relaxed again. Now that he knew, it all fell into place. Her name was Yasmin. The first poster had shown her dressed in a black jacket and fishnet tights. She was holding a top hat in one hand while she kept a group of lions at bay with a whip. In the second she had been flying through the air high above the ring holding on to a trapeze by one foot. They were both artist's impressions, and no doubt he'd given full rein to his imagination, but the likeness was there.

She must be doing well to be driving a nearly new BMW. It was intriguing. He had never met a circus artist before. If the advertisements were anything to go by, no wonder she oozed confidence.

'You are a girl of many parts.'

She shrugged. 'In a small travelling circus like ours you have to be. We all do many things.' For a moment she relaxed and became animated again.

'I would like to come and see you.'

By now they were almost in the middle of the town. The harbour lay to the right and through an alleyway he caught a glimpse of the sea.

'That would be nice. Look . . .' She pulled up sharply. 'I am afraid I shan't be able to take you to your hotel after all. I must drop you here.'

'*D'accord*. It was kind of you to bring us this far.' He wanted to say more, but for the first time on the journey he felt tongue-tied.

'Please hurry.' She stared back the way they had come and he saw an expression almost of fear in her eyes. She suddenly looked very small and vulnerable.

'Of course.' He was out of the car in a flash. Ever alert to his master's wishes, Pommes Frites followed suit.

Monsieur Pamplemousse paused as he shut the door. 'Thank you once again. If I can be of any help, at any time, I shall be at the Ty Coz. You know my name. You can leave a message.'

'Thank you.' She sounded genuinely grateful and he wondered if she would indeed take up the offer.

He hardly had time to shut the boot before she was on her way again. The BMW disappeared round the next corner, towards the harbour, just as the van came into view. As it slowed to negotiate the intersection he caught a glimpse of the driver. Around his neck was a gold cross on a chain. Their eyes met for a brief second and Pamplemousse knew he had seen him somewhere before. The van was on hire. It was a Renault with a local registration. Taking out his notebook he flipped through the pages and added its number to the day's notes. It might be worth a telephone call when he got to the hotel.

The garage next to the *Mairie* was closed, but if his memory served him right there used to be one near the harbour which refuelled the fishermen's boats as well. In those days he hadn't owned a car. He and Doucette had taken the train to St. Nazaire and then caught the *autobus*. It had been a big adventure. He looked at his watch again. It was twenty to seven, but the garage might still be open. It was worth a try.

Feeling out of place in his Paris suit, Monsieur Pample-mousse gathered up the luggage and set off, his thoughts still very much on the girl. Reminders of her were pasted up everywhere, on walls and telegraph poles.

Following on behind, Pommes Frites wore his resigned expression. He knew the signs. His master was smitten.

When they reached the harbour it became clear that all the action was at the other end of the promenade. The circus was located on a patch of scrubland a little way back from the beach. The 'big top', shielded from the prevailing wind by a group of caravans and lorries, was festooned with coloured lights. A low-pitched continuous grinding sound interspersed with the spasmodic crack of rifle-fire could be heard from the fairground alongside it. He wondered how many other parts the girl played. Perhaps even now she was already drumming up custom for the hoop-la. It was a hard life.

The Quai Jules Verne was as he remembered it, except it was now called Quai Général de Gaulle. In fairness, the latter had a better claim. Jules Verne had only once in his life been to Port St. Augustin, and that only on a school outing from his home town of Nantes.

The old cobbled street leading back to the centre of town now had a 'No Entry' sign. It had been turned into a shop-ping precinct. The cobbles had been re-laid and everywhere there were concrete tubs filled with flowers. It was lined on either side with expensive-looking boutiques displaying the latest Paris fashions. There was even a bookshop.

Benches were dotted along the promenade, sandwiched between waste bins whose black plastic liners peeped out from beneath garish orange lids.

Three nuns came towards him. It was a good omen. To meet one or more was supposed to bring good fortune, provided you didn't see their backs. Three was especially lucky. It would make up for the earlier episode. He let them go past.

Much to his relief, the garage was still there. And it was open. Apart from a row of modern pumps, it had hardly changed. In the old days they had been worked by hand.

'*Pas de problème, Monsieur.*' The owner seemed only too pleased at the prospect of an evening job outside the town. He would finish what he was doing – ten minutes at the most – then he would take *Monsieur* to his hotel, go and collect the car before it got dark and deliver it later that night. Yes, he had heard good reports of the Ty Coz, but it was not for local people. It was for the tourists.

Monsieur Pamplemousse was tempted to stroll along to the end of the promenade in order to have a quick look at the circus, but he decided instead to spend the time looking round the tiny port. Tomorrow evening would be soon enough.

A new car-park had been built and was chock-a-block. There were also many more yachts in the harbour than he remembered, the smaller ones moving gently on the swell from the incoming tide. In the old days it had been full of fishing boats. The local florist must do well. The larger the yacht, the bigger the investment in flowers. Some of them looked too immaculate and lived-in ever to put to sea.

The waitresses in the Hôtel du Port were getting ready for dinner, their starched *coiffes* bobbing up and down as they bent over the tables. There would probably be a rush of early diners wanting to go to the circus afterwards. The Hôtel now boasted an enormous electrically operated blind to protect those facing westward from the setting sun. The bathrooms would have expensive tiles and the latest plumbing. At least the dark, solid, old-fashioned Breton furniture was still there. It was probably too heavy to move and no one else would want it anyway. It summed up modern France in a way. One foot firmly planted in the twenty-first century, the other deeply rooted in the past. In Paris uniformed men riding *Caninettes* searched the pavements for evidence of canine misdemeanours – Pommes Frites led a hunted life these days: he could hardly call his *merde* his own – while their colleagues looking after the gutters still used rolls of old carpet tied up with string to divert the water which gushed down every day from the heights of Montmartre, for the very simple reason that no one had come up with a better idea. It was the same here. The old public wash-house was still intact and looked well used, but the *pissotière* had been replaced by a concrete and steel *Sanisette*. Its predecessor had smelled to high heaven in August – worse than the fish market – but at least it had been free. Not that financial considerations seemed to make any difference these days. As he strolled past it a man carrying a small brown valise slipped a coin in the slot and stood waiting. There was a brief snatch of music as the door slid open and then closed behind him. Everything was done to music these days. Even *Le Guide* had been forced to introduce a symbol for piped music in restaurants, a loudspeaker rampant.

Monsieur Pamplemousse suddenly paused in his musings, hardly able to believe his eyes. On one of the benches further along the promenade, deeply immersed in a *journal*, sat a familiar figure. It hardly seemed possible, and yet, come to think of it, why not? Brittany was very much a home from home for lots of English families, some of whom took their holidays there year after year. It had always been that way. He well remembered their strange habit of marking the level of wine left in the bottle before they went upstairs to bed at night. He'd always thought of it as 'the English habit', although he'd since learnt it was far from typical.

A feeling of excitement came over him and he quickened

his pace. Although they had spoken on the telephone several times – notably when he'd been involved in the case of the missing girls at the finishing school near Evian – it was a long time since they last met. Three years? Four?

He almost broke into a trot as he covered the last few metres, his hand extended.

'Monsieur Pickering. How good to see you! *Comment ça va?*'

The figure on the bench glanced up from his *journal*, then looked briefly at his wrist-watch.

'*C'est dix-sept plus cinq minutes.*' It was said in a flat monotone, almost devoid of expression. Having imparted the information, the owner of the voice pointedly returned to his crossword.

'But . . .' Monsieur Pamplemousse hardly knew what to say. 'It *is* Monsieur Pickering, *n'est-ce pas*? Surely you remember me?'

'Look, piss off, there's a good chap.' This time the words came through clenched teeth and were said with such feeling Monsieur Pamplemousse practically reeled back as if he had been hit.

As he made his way slowly back along the promenade he felt totally shattered; rejected on all sides. First there had been the accident with his car, then the girl. Now, Mr. Pickering – someone he had always looked on as a friend – had denied him.

So much for *entente cordiale*. Anything less *cordiale* than Mr. Pickering's reception would be hard to imagine.

Feeling Pommes Frites nuzzle up against him, he reached down and patted his head. At least, come rain or shine, you knew where you stood with Pommes Frites. His was no fair weather friendship.

He directed his thoughts towards Ty Coz. When they got there they would have a good meal to make up for it. It would be a meal to end all meals; no expense spared. There would be no stinting. Madame Grante would have a fit when she saw *l'addition*. He could picture it all.

But as he crossed the road towards the garage, something else happened which gave him cause for thought. He was not unfamiliar with the workings of *Sanisettes*. Indeed, following his experience in St. Georges-sur-Lie when for a brief period he had been incarcerated in one while inspecting an hotel belonging to the Director's Aunt Louise, he'd become a walking mine of information on the technicalities of their workings.

Efficient, they might be. A minor miracle of electronics as applied to public facilities, yes. Sanitised, certainly. But fast, no. The cleaning cycle following each operation alone took exactly forty seconds, so there was no question of one out, the next one in.

And therein lay the nub of the matter. His encounter with Mr. Pickering had been brief and to the point; it had certainly taken not longer than a minute or so. And yet he'd been barely halfway across the road when the door to the *Sanisette* slid open and out came a nun. Moreover, she was carrying a small brown valise.

Clearly, the undercurrents in St. Augustin were not restricted to rocking the boats in the port. Some were hard at work on land as well.

3

TRUFFLE TROUBLE

Removing a box bearing a large red cross from the leather case provided by *Le Guide* as standard issue to all its Inspectors, Monsieur Pamplemousse opened it and began looking for a tube of antiseptic ointment and a plaster. For the latter he needed one which was both generous in its measurements and in its powers of adhesion, for Pommes Frites' nose was, to say the least, not only large but usually very wet, and he wouldn't be at all happy if the plaster fell off into his breakfast. Not that the thought of breakfast at the Ty Coz was uppermost in either of their minds at that moment. If their experience of the previous evening was anything to go by, their fast would best be broken elsewhere.

In designing the original case, which had changed very little in its basic concept over the years, the founder of *Le Guide*, Monsieur Hippolyte Duval – a perfectionist in all that he did – had sought to provide for any emergency likely to be encountered by members of his staff whilst in the field.

Monsieur Pamplemousse couldn't help but reflect as he discarded first one and then another plaster as being either too small or the wrong shape, that Monsieur Duval had probably never envisaged the need to come to the rescue of a bloodhound who had suffered injury to his proboscis from the business end of a ball-point pen, or indeed any sort of pen –

given the fact that the ball-point wasn't invented until long after the Founder had passed on.

Monsieur Pamplemousse felt terrible. He would far sooner have speared his own nose than wound Pommes Frites' in the way that he had. Had he been brought up in court by an animal protection society, his excuse would have sounded very lame indeed. His head bowed in shame.

The previous evening had been an unrelieved disaster. The only good thing that had happened was the retrieval of his car, looking none the worse for its adventure. One more tribute to a design which in many respects was hard to fault.

The food in the hotel restaurant had turned out to be unbelievably bad. How the other diners could get through their meal, some with every appearance of enjoyment, was beyond him. Not even several measures of a particularly vicious Calvados had entirely taken away the salty taste. Since the bottle had been without a label he strongly suspected the chef must make it himself during the long winter evenings.

In the end he and Pommes Frites had retired to bed early armed with a large supply of Evian, the seals of the bottles unbroken to make sure the contents hadn't been tampered with. After a long drive he had hoped they might both get a good night's sleep. But hunger proved to be a poor bed-fellow. Apart from which he had many things on his mind.

Mr. Pickering's strange behaviour kept him occupied for quite a while; he couldn't for the life of him think what he might have said or done to cause his old friend to act the way he had. The goings-on in the *Sanisette* were something else again. Coupled with the behaviour of the nuns in the car earlier in the day, he began to wonder whether he wasn't witnessing the total decline of the Catholic Church; the Pope must be a very worried *homme*. Thinking about the girl who had given him a lift only added to his restlessness – he couldn't get the sudden change in her behaviour out of his mind; one moment so cool and sure of herself, the next moment clearly afraid. But afraid of what? Magnified as such thoughts always are in the hours of darkness, he began to wish he'd gone to the circus after all, picturing himself in the role of rescuer from whatever it was that was troubling her.

He tried counting sheep, but that only made matters worse. They all wore frilly white collars, the kind used to decorate roast crown of lamb. He pushed the thought aside.

Last, but not least, there was the task which had brought him to Port St. Augustin in the first place: catering for the inaugural flight of the airship. Switching on the bedside light, he reached for his pen and pad. For one reason and another he hadn't even begun to think of a possible menu and time wasn't on his side. Neither as it happened, was inspiration. One thing was certain, he wouldn't find it by staying at the Ty Coz. Why on earth the Director had insisted on his going there he would never know.

In desperation he sought refuge in a game popularly known to himself and his colleagues on *Le Guide* as 'The Last Supper'. It was one they played on those occasions when they were able to meet up *en masse* as it were; the annual staff outing at the Director's weekend retreat in Normandy perhaps, or when things were comparatively slack after the March launch and they were all in the office getting ready for the next edition.

Over the years they had played it so many times the result was a foregone conclusion, but it was no less enjoyable for all that, giving rise to much smacking of lips and to reminiscences which often went on far into the night.

Monsieur Pamplemousse's own choice on such occasions was clear and uncompromising. Simplicity was the keynote. Truffle soup at Bocuse's restaurant just outside Lyon. A simple grilled *filet* steak – preferably from a Charolais bull – accompanied by a green salad, at any one of a hundred restaurants he could have named without even stopping to think; followed, if heavenly dispensation made it possible to arrange, by *pommes frites* cooked by the *patron* of a little hillside café he'd once come across on the D942 west of Carpentras; light, crisp, golden, piping hot, and always served as a separate course, for they were perfection in their own right. The wine would be an Hermitage from Monsieur Chave, and after the cheese – the final choice would depend on the time of the year – a *tarte aux pommes légère*, wafer thin, and topped with equally thin slivers of almond.

His salivary glands working overtime, Monsieur Pamplemousse lay awake for a long time after that. If he were to expire during the night – and the way he felt, such an event was not entirely outside the bounds of possibility – it would not be as a happy man.

And so it came to pass that with food uppermost in his mind, he fell into a fitful sleep, dreaming, perhaps not unsurprisingly in the circumstances, of what might have been.

However, as he settled down to enjoy the meal of his dreams something very strange happened. A ton weight seemed to have settled on his stomach, pinning him to the bed. The more he struggled the harder it became to move, and panic set in.

Then, just as he was about to give up all hope of rescue, a waiter appeared bearing not the expected bowl of soup, but what could only be described as a kit of parts; a platter of pastry, a jug containing chicken stock, and a plate on which reposed a single black truffle – a magnificent specimen to be sure, the biggest he had ever seen – twice the size of a large walnut. Madame Grante would have had a fit if she'd seen it.

He reached forward to pick it up. But the surface was moist and as soon as his fingers made contact it shot out from between them and rolled across the table cloth, hovering for a moment or two before settling down again. He tried a second time, then a third, but on each occasion the result was the same. The truffle seemed to have a life of its own.

Stealth was needed. Glancing over his shoulder to make sure no one was watching, Monsieur Pamplemousse clasped his pen. Then he made a lightning stab at the object in front of him.

Alonzo T. Cross, inventor of the world's first propelling pencil – a forerunner of Monsieur Pamplemousse's present weapon – would have been well satisfied with the result, for it was a tribute to the sharpness of his products.

Not even a banshee, that spirit of Celtic superstition reputed to howl beneath the window of a house where the occupant is about to die, could have surpassed the cry which rent the air as the finely engineered point of the pen made contact with its target.

Monsieur Pamplemousse woke with a start and found himself lying half on and half off his hotel bed, with Pommes Frites eyeing him dolefully, not to say fearfully, from the other side of the room. He wore an expression, as well he might in the circumstances, of a dog who has just suffered the ultimate betrayal of a love which he had always assumed would last forever. To make matters worse it had happened at the very moment when he'd been in the middle of showing his affection for his master with a morning lick. St. Hubert – the patron saint of bloodhounds – would have been outraged had he been present at the scene.

As Monsieur Pamplemousse looked at the end of his pen and then at Pommes Frites' nose, he realised for the first time that the latter bore a distinct resemblance to the *Tuber menosporum* of his dreams and remorse immediately set in. Pommes Frites' proboscis, once the pride and joy of the *Sûreté*, follower to the bitter end of many a trail, sometime winner of the Pierre Armand trophy for the best sniffer dog of his year, was not something to be trifled with. Its impairment would be almost as hard to bear for those who in one way or another depended on its proper functioning as it would be for Pommes Frites himself. Reports for *Le Guide* would suffer. Tastings in restaurants across the length and breadth of France would lose their authority.

As he applied a generous helping of ointment to the end of Pommes Frites' olfactory organ and then pressed a plaster firmly into place, anger filled Monsieur Pamplemousse's soul. One look at the expression in his friend's eyes confirmed in him the need for action no matter what the consequences.

Replacing the first aid box in the case, he reached for the

tray containing the camera equipment, then paused for a moment. It was tempting to take a picture of his patient for use in case there were any arguments later. But that would be unkind; it would be rubbing salt into the wound, and salt was the one culinary item any mention of which was strictly taboo for the time being.

Monsieur Pamplemousse came to a decision. Enough was enough. In this instance, more than enough. He picked up another, much larger case and placed it on the bed.

Recognising the signs, Pommes Frites wagged his tail. The possibility of spending any more time in their present surroundings was not something he could enthuse over either. Normally he had great faith in his master's ability to turn up trumps when it came to finding places to stay, but that too had undergone a severe shaking.

A few minutes later they drove out of the hotel car-park and joined the queue of traffic already heading for the beach.

As the sea came into view Pommes Frites put his head out through the open window on the passenger side and sniffed. He immediately wished he hadn't. Exhaust fumes rather than ozone filled the air; that, and a strong smell of ointment. Neither was pleasant on an empty stomach. The automatic seat belt alongside Monsieur Pamplemousse tightened as they negotiated the roundabout in the centre of the town and Pommes Frites settled back in his seat.

But if Pommes Frites was looking forward to a gambol on the sands followed by a dip in the ocean, he was disappointed. His master had other priorities. Pulling up alongside a row of telephone *cabines* at the far end of the promenade, Monsieur Pamplemousse signalled Pommes Frites to wait.

Flicking open his wallet as he entered the nearest *cabine*, he withdrew a blue plastic card from its protective covering and committed it to a slot in front of him. Sliding shut the small black door in the apparatus he pressed a series of buttons appropriate to his call; the 16-1 code for Paris, followed by a further eight digits. He noted that nineteen of the original forty units on his *Télécarte* were still available. Provided he didn't have too many interruptions they should allow him more than enough time to give vent to his feelings. During the drive from the hotel he had marshalled his thoughts into their appropriate order, rehearsing out loud his end of the conversation, honing it and polishing it until he was word perfect. Even though he hadn't understood a word, Pommes Frites had got the gist and he'd looked suitably impressed.

'*Le Guide. Puis-je vous aider?*' A familiar voice responded before the second ring was complete.

'Ah, Véronique. *Monsieur le Directeur, s'il vous plaît.*'

'Monsieur Pamplemousse! How are you? And how is the weather in Brittany?'

'The weather in Brittany,' said Monsieur Pamplemousse, 'is *très bien*. I, unfortunately, am not. I am far from *bien*.' He kept a watchful eye on the digital counter. Véronique was a nice girl, but he had little time at his disposal for pleasantries. He was short of change and he didn't want to spend time looking for somewhere to buy another *carte*.

Something in the tone of his voice must have conveyed itself via the many cables and amplifiers linking the western coast of France with the seventh *arrondissement* in Paris. Nuances of urgency had not been attenuated *en route*.

'I will put you through at once, *Monsieur*.'

Monsieur Pamplemousse murmured his thanks and waited, growing steadily more impatient with every passing second. Clearly the Director was not poised, as his secretary had been, in readiness to receive incoming calls.

He glanced across the road while he was waiting. A police car was parked outside the circus, but there was no sign of the occupants. Two men were busy setting up the *carrousel*. To the side of one of the caravans a woman was hanging out a line of washing. There was no sign of the girl, Yasmin, although he could see her car parked alongside a big generating lorry near the back. Behind the car, somewhat incongruously, there was a large menhir – one of the many 'great stones' bequeathed to that part of Brittany by a people who had inhabited the land even before the Gauls had come upon the scene.

Looking towards the port he considered the possibility that he might see Mr. Pickering, but the road was empty. Nearly everyone was down on the sand. A low stone wall separated the beach from the promenade, at the same time sheltering beds of late spring flowers from the prevailing wind. That too, was new. Beyond a beflagged sign bearing the words *Centre Sportif* children's heads rose into view, hovered momentarily, then disappeared again as their owners bounced up and down on a trampoline. Further down the beach other small figures were hard at work building sandcastles, anxious to complete them before they were enveloped by the incoming tide. He guessed they must be English. An insular race, the English, always digging themselves in. Their insularity and desire to conquer started at an early age. Even as he watched, one of them confirmed his suspicions by adding a Union Jack to one of the battlements. A provocative gesture on foreign soil – especially as he must have brought it with him with that sole purpose in mind.

A late fishing boat chugged its way towards the harbour, an escort of gulls wheeling and screeching overhead. An old biplane came into view, towing a banner. Shielding his eyes against the sun, he made out the word *cirque*.

'Aristide, how are you? And how is the weather in Brittany?' It was the Director at last, sounding slightly out of breath. Did his voice also contain a hint of anxiety? A suggestion of trepidation?

Monsieur Pamplemousse repeated the reply he had given Véronique, but with even greater emphasis.

'Oh, dear. I am sorry to hear that, Aristide. I was hoping the change of air would do you good. May I ask what is wrong?'

'I can give you the answer in three words, *Monsieur. Cuisine Régionale Naturelle.*'

'Don't tell me you are tired of fish already, Pamplemousse. I find that hard to believe.' The Director assumed his censorious voice. 'You have only been at Ty Coz a matter of hours.

48

Hardly time to unpack your valise.'

'My valise, *Monsieur*, is in the back of my car, and there it will remain until Pommes Frites and I have found another hotel.'

'But, Aristide, is this not a trifle premature? It is a plum assignment. *Cuisine Régionale Naturelle* is, after all, an entirely new technique. If we are to consider it for inclusion in *Le Guide*, extensive field trials will be necessary. I hesitate to say this, but it is a well known fact that our taste buds diminish in number as we grow older. One has to persevere, however . . .'

'Mine will disappear altogether if I stay at Ty Coz,' said Monsieur Pamplemousse. 'They will have been pickled for posterity.'

'Come, come, Aristide. This is not like you. As with all new things, *Cuisine Régionale Naturelle* is doubtless an acquired taste.' There was a definite note of panic in the Director's voice.

'Then someone else will have to acquire it, *Monsieur*. Guilot, for example. He is always trying to lose weight. He might welcome the chance to go without food for a while.'

Over the telephone he heard the distinct sound of a cork being withdrawn from a bottle. It was followed by a 'glugging' noise. He braced himself for the attack. It was not long in coming.

'Pamplemousse. Nothing grieves me more than to have to put the matter this way, but I am afraid it is no longer a request. It is a command. Accommodation has been reserved at Ty Coz until the day after the launch. Your flag is firmly placed on the map of France in the operations room. I must warn you here and now that if you go elsewhere not only will opprobrium fall upon your head but I shall be unable to justify your P39s to Madame Grante . . .'

Monsieur Pamplemousse took a deep breath as he cut across the Director's monologue, but with only five units left on his card it was essential to get his point across.

'*Monsieur*, have you tried eating *Cuisine Régionale*

Naturelle?'

'I am told it is very popular in Okinawa, Aristide . . .' Clearly the Director was not giving in without a fight. Monsieur Pamplemousse resisted the temptation to remark that it confirmed his worst suspicions. Whoever had recommended the hotel couldn't possibly have been a Frenchman. An oriental with a grudge perhaps?

'There are doubtless many things not to our taste which are popular in Okinawa, *Monsieur.*' In deference to Pommes Frites he turned and lowered his voice. '*Chiens en croûte* are probably considered a delicacy, whereas over here . . .'

He paused.

Along the road nearer the port a man on a ladder was pasting a white paper across one of the circus posters.

'It is also possible that the waters of the Pacific are less polluted than those of the Atlantic Ocean, but even if that is true I doubt if they cook everything in sea-water. Fish is not the only speciality of the region, *Monsieur.* The Guérande peninsula is also the centre for salt production . . .' Even by hanging outside the *cabine* he couldn't read the label.

'Everything? But that is not possible!'

'*Tout à fait, Monsieur.* Everything at Ty Coz is either cooked in or made with sea-water. The bread, the mayonnaise, even the coffee. Had we stayed for breakfast, I am sure even the dough for the *croissants* would have been mixed with sea-water. Pommes Frites was sick twice yesterday evening and he is not normally one to complain.

'The final straw came when I mistook the end of his nose for a truffle.'

A nun zoomed past on a *cyclomoteur*, a brace of *baguettes* clipped to the rear pannier. Monsieur Pamplemousse gave a start. He could have sworn he'd caught a glimpse of rolled-up trousers beneath her black skirt as it billowed in the slipstream. He crossed himself as he followed her progress along the promenade.

'Pamplemousse, are you there? Can you hear me? Did you say a *truffle*? Frankly, I am worried about you. Was the roof of your car open on the journey down yesterday? One forgets the sun can be strong at this time of the year.'

'*Pardon, Monsieur.* I was distracted momentarily. A nun went past on a motorised cycle. Her habit was caught in the slipstream and I couldn't help noticing what she was wearing underneath . . .'

There was a moment's silence. 'Pamplemousse! I sometimes despair, I really do. Is there no end to your depravity? Is there nothing that can assuage your desires of the flesh? A poor girl who has forsaken all to take the vow?' Once again there was a distinct sound of something being poured from a bottle. 'Was she – was she a young novice, perhaps? I must confess, I have often wondered about these things myself.'

'*Monsieur*, whatever else she was, I suspect she was no novice, nor was she particularly young.'

'Age is immaterial, Pamplemousse. It is the principle. Or rather, the lack of principle. It is . . .' There was a click and the line went dead.

Feeling that it had somehow been a less than satisfactory conversation, not quite as rehearsed, Monsieur Pamplemousse replaced the handset and left the *cabine*. Perhaps in the end if accommodation was difficult he would compromise by keeping his room at the Ty Coz and eating out. But at least he had made his point.

He hesitated for a moment. The man with the ladder was now working on another poster – slightly nearer this time. He wondered whether to take a closer look, then glanced at his watch. It showed barely a quarter to ten. His rendezvous with the airship wasn't until eleven. There would be time to take a quick look at the circus – perhaps even reserve a seat for the evening's performance – before strolling along to one of the cafés near the harbour for a leisurely breakfast. He must also remember to get a card for Doucette. That was always one of his first acts on arriving anywhere. She would start to worry if he didn't.

Pommes Frites jumped out of the car and followed his master across the road with alacrity. There was a lot to catch up on.

Monsieur Pamplemousse led the way towards the back of the waste ground. Close to, the BMW looked even more incongruous against the menhir; the blue van parked on the other side of it hardly less so. He wondered idly what the early inhabitants who had struggled to erect the stone all those thousands of years ago would think if they could see it now. No doubt they would marvel at the BMW, just as today's inhabitants marvelled at the stone. Both attracted their worshippers.

Pommes Frites had no such respect for antiquity. For some reason best known to himself he appeared to have taken a violent dislike to the menhir. Having run round and round it several times growling and barking, he then bestowed his mark, not as a sign of favour, but rather the reverse, sniffing the stone at the same time, thus leaving behind a strong smell of embrocation as well. The previous evening's meal had given rise to a great thirst during the night, and Pommes Frites was clearly in no hurry.

While he was waiting, Monsieur Pamplemousse looked around. He had a strange, almost eerie sensation of being watched, but there was no one about. The whole site seemed strangely quiet. The doors to the motley collection of caravans were nearly all closed; the blinds drawn. There was no sign of the woman with the washing he'd noticed earlier. The line of side shows still had their shutters up. No doubt when the lights were on and there were people around it was all very different, but by daylight it simply looked tatty. Tatty and rather sad. The old Gustave Bayol *carrousel* had seen better days, although nothing would ever replace the quality of the delicately carved horses with their rosettes and tassels. It must have been someone's pride and joy when it was new.

He wandered along through the fairground towards the circus tent, past the Dodgem cars and a heavily ornamented caravan belonging to a fortune-teller, its sides covered in paintings of stars and other heavenly bodies. Next to the caravan were two tents, one of which had a Jacques Courtois painted canvas façade advertising the only bearded lady left in Europe, the other bore a picture depicting the smallest man in the world. Both tents had their flaps tightly closed. Next came a coconut shy, and after that a helter-skelter.

He could smell the circus long before he reached it; a mixture of sawdust and animals. It was the same smell he had noticed in the girl's car.

Some Arab ponies were tethered to a tree, and near by there was a cage containing an elderly lion. It was fast asleep, enjoying the sunshine. Clearly, it suffered from the kind of affliction even its best friend wouldn't have mentioned. But who would tell a lion? Seeing something lying on the ground, he stooped and picked it up. It was a small piece of fibreglass, newly sawn – the cut was still shiny. From force of habit he slipped it into his pocket.

To his right lay the entrance to the 'big top', fronted by a decorated pay-box. He made his way across the down-trodden grass. It was worth a try. But once again he drew a blank, and he was about to give up when he heard someone call out.

A man appeared from behind a lorry, eyeing him suspiciously. 'What do you want? We're not open yet.'

'I was wanting a ticket for the circus.'

'The *matinée* has been cancelled.'

'Tonight will be fine.'

'Tonight! *Pas de problème*! You can have as many as you like. *Vingt, cinquante, cent* . . .'

'I want one only.'

'Poof!' The man raised his hands. Clearly he had better things to do than open up the box office just for the sake of selling one ticket. He pointed towards the fortune teller's caravan. 'You'd better see Madame Caoutchouc. She's the boss.'

Monsieur Pamplemousse made his way back across the fairground, threading a path through the stalls and sideshows until he reached the caravan. Signalling Pommes Frites to wait outside, he climbed the steps and knocked on the door. There was no reply. After a moment or two he turned the handle and pushed it open.

He found himself in a small area curtained off by black drapes hanging from rails fixed to the ceiling. In the middle there was a round, baize-covered table in the centre of which stood a large crystal ball. There were two chairs – one just inside the door, the other on the far side. A single shaded lamp suspended from the roof threw a pool of light onto the table.

Monsieur Pamplemousse called out, but again there was no reply. Pulling the curtain on his left to one side revealed a bedroom. A built-in bed occupied most of the space and to one side of it there was another door. It was reminiscent of a ship's cabin or the sleeping-berth on an overnight express train – all polished wood and brass. Underneath the bed he could see what looked like a long leather bag. On top of the bed there was a red cushion embroidered with a piano keyboard.

He tried parting the curtains on the other side. It was a real old-fashioned Showman's caravan and no mistake. A long bow-fronted sideboard ran along one wall. The top was covered with knick-knacks collected during a lifetime of travel, old photographs in silver frames, china and brass ornaments. They must all be stowed away when the circus was on the move and brought out again at each place of call. In the centre of the sideboard, looking totally out of place, there was a Sony hi-fi – all black dials and knobs, with two miniature loudspeakers, one on either side. On the wall behind it there was a large old-fashioned mirror with a patterned border etched into the glass. On a small table in the centre of the room there was a vase full of fresh flowers, and along the remaining wall a small sink and a cooking stove let into the top of some fitted cupboards.

It was someone's whole world encapsulated in a few square metres.

It certainly wouldn't have done for Doucette, nor for him either. He found himself wondering what Madame Caoutchouc did in her spare moments – other than listen to the radio. There wasn't a single book or a magazine to be seen anywhere. His own day was rarely complete without reading something before he went to sleep. Perhaps she didn't have any spare moments.

At that moment he heard footsteps coming up the steps. He let the curtain fall back into place and turned just as the door opened.

If Madame Caoutchouc was surprised to see such an early customer she hardly registered the fact. Instead she motioned him towards the nearest chair.

She looked worried, distracted. He could see the family likeness at once. She was an older, larger version of the girl. Yasmin in perhaps twenty years' time.

'I have told you all I know. There is nothing more to add.'

Monsieur Pamplemousse looked suitably baffled.

'I'm sorry. I do not understand . . .'

It was Madame Caoutchouc's turn to look confused.

'You are not from the press?'

He shook his head.

'Or the police?'

He shook his head again. 'No. I simply wanted to buy a ticket for tonight's performance.'

Madame Caoutchouc gave a short laugh. 'Tonight? To-night, there will be no problem, *Monsieur*.' She reached for the door handle.

Monsieur Pamplemousse shrugged. For reasons best known to themselves, Le Cirque Bretagno was not in the business of selling tickets that morning. So be it. He turned and was about to leave when the memory of the man pasting over the advertising posters came back to him.

'I'm sorry. I do not understand. There *is* a show tonight?'

There was moment's hesitation. 'You mean you haven't heard about the accident? *Morbleu!*'

Monsieur Pamplemousse felt an icy hand clutching at the pit of his stomach. He knew the answer before he even posed the question.

'It was the trapeze artiste? The girl Yasmin?'

Madame Caoutchouc nodded. 'It was terrible. I was there when it happened. I saw it all. There was nothing anyone could do. She missed the bar after a triple somersault. It was a difficult trick, but she had done it many times before. She landed in the net – that too, has happened many times – but this time . . .' She suddenly had difficulty in finding the right words.

'We did everything we could. Everything. I went with her in the ambulance . . .'

Monsieur Pamplemousse asked the question uppermost in his mind.

'No, she isn't dead, but she is in a coma. If you had seen her lying there . . .'

To his dismay Madame Caoutchouc suddenly burst into a flood of tears. It was as though a dam had broken. For a moment or two it was so uncontrollable he felt at a loss to know what to do or say. It was always the same when he was confronted by a woman crying; a mixture of tenderness and helplessness, which occasionally gave way to irrational anger, not with the person concerned, but with his own inability to supply the right words.

'I am sorry.' He reached out and touched her. 'If there is anything I can do.' For a moment he was tempted to tell Madame Caoutchouc about his meeting with the girl, then he decided against it. There seemed little point.

'*Merci, Monsieur.*' With a struggle she pulled herself together. 'I'm sorry. I am a little overwrought. The police have been here asking questions. What do they know about the circus?

'There will be a show tonight – we cannot afford not to have one, but it will be without Yasmin. And without Yasmin, I think there will be no problem about tickets.'

'*Merci, Madame.*' He held her hand briefly, then turned to go. 'I am sorry to have troubled you. I did not realise what had happened.'

Madame Caoutchouc followed him to the door. Halfway down the steps Monsieur Pamplemousse paused and looked back at her.

'You say you went with your daughter to the hospital? Did she – did she say anything while you were there? Anything at all?'

'A few words in the ambulance, that is all. And they were a struggle. Nothing that made sense. I think she must have been delirious by then.'

'Do you remember what she said?'

He immediately regretted asking the question. For a moment or two it looked as though Madame Caoutchouc was about to burst into tears again, then she recovered herself.

'It was just the one word. It sounded like *pamplemousse*. *Pamplemousse, pamplemousse, pamplemousse,* she kept repeating it over and over again. Who knows what she was trying to say?'

'Who knows?' said Monsieur Pamplemousse. 'Who indeed knows?'

4

THE SIX GLORIES OF FRANCE

Leaving his car parked outside the telephone *cabines*, Monsieur Pamplemousse walked slowly back along the beach towards the harbour. The wind had started to freshen, but he hardly noticed it. He was sunk in gloom. He could still hardly believe the news about the girl's accident. There was probably nothing at all that he could have done to help her, and yet somehow he couldn't rid himself of a feeling of being in some way partly responsible. If only he had gone to see her the night before, perhaps it wouldn't have happened. Perhaps she'd had her mind on some problem and that in turn had caused a momentary loss of concentration. He was glad he hadn't seen her fall. That would have been too awful in the circumstances. Sensing his mood, Pommes Frites presented him with a stick he'd found. It was a specially large one with some seaweed attached.

When they reached the port Monsieur Pamplemousse bought a postcard for Doucette in a shop which sold everything from fishing nets to wooden *sabots*, via Breton lace, hand-painted china, and oilskins – a reminder that Brittany had 'weather' – even in summer. The card showed a man paddling a flat-bottomed boat through the local marshes; it was a choice between that, views of the harbour, the salt pans, or close-up pictures of lobsters awaiting the pot.

Coming out of the shop the first thing he saw was a picture of the girl. Her face looked out at him from the front page of a local *journal*. They must have worked quickly. He bought a copy and led the way to a café a little way along the front.

Suddenly realising how hungry he was, he ordered a *crêpe au sucre* as well as a plate of *croissants*, a large cup of *chocolat*, and a bowl of water for Pommes Frites. Then, to the sound of halyards slapping against steel masts in the freshening wind, he settled down to read the *journal*.

In the end it didn't tell him much more than he already knew, or could have guessed. Le Cirque Bretagno was a small family-owned concern of Italian origin that had been going the rounds since before the turn of the century, handed down from father to son and currently being run by the mother. The father had died several years ago. It travelled all over Europe, seldom staying more than a night or two in any one place, and only intended being in Port St. Augustin for three nights before heading further south towards Bordeaux.

The accident had happened when Yasmin was performing a change-over on the high trapeze. It was a difficult manoeuvre – the high-spot of the act – but one which she had performed many times. No one knew quite what went wrong; a momentary loss of concentration, a split-second error of judgement; her hands had touched the other bar, but too late to tighten her grip. With such a trick there was no second chance. It underlined the ever present danger of circus life, and the fact that even with a safety net disasters could happen. Tragedy was never far away, lurking round the next corner waiting for a chance to strike. But nowadays people were so blasé; they had seen such tricks many times before on television.

Yasmin was twenty-eight. She was still in a coma, but the local hospital hoped to issue a statement after she had undergone further examination. Her temporary loss was a great blow to the circus, but they would do their best to carry on.

Monsieur Pamplemousse folded the paper carefully, broke the remaining *croissant* in two and gave one piece to Pommes Frites, then he signalled for the bill. The clock on the church tower said ten-forty. It was time they were on their way.

Back in the car, he unlocked his issue case and removed the Leica camera and the Trinovid binoculars. The flight would give him a good opportunity to take some aerial photographs; something he had never done before. He hovered over the compartments of the felt-lined tray for a moment or two, unable to make up his mind which lenses to take, but eventually settled on the standard 50mm and the 28mm wide-angle. He had no idea how high they might be flying and he wished now he'd given the matter more thought; there might be a problem with the light. He always kept ultra-violet filters on the lenses anyway; they provided extra protection against scratches, but he slipped a couple of yellow filters into his jacket pocket to be on the safe side.

On the spur of the moment and acting on an impulse that had paid off many times in his days with the Force, he attached an auto-wind to the camera, slipped a zoom lens into place, and on the pretext of checking it, pointed the camera in the direction of the circus and shot off the rest of the reel of film. As far as he could tell, no one had seen him do it. A few moments later, the camera re-loaded, they set off.

The airship was tethered to a mooring-mast attached to the back of a large lorry. From a distance it looked like a giant wind-sock floating to and fro, the double wheels below the gondola describing a large arc as the wind blew the envelope first one way and then the other. There were more people standing around waiting for his arrival than he expected. No doubt they all had a function to perform, but it reminded him of a film set, with everyone poised for action. On the other hand, security struck him as being remarkably lax; apart from two gendarmes and a man in civilian clothes occupying a hut at the entrance to the field, no one asked to see his credentials and he was allowed to drive right up to the concrete square which served as a landing and take-off area. If the dark grey pill-boxes near the cliffs were anything to go by it was probably a relic of the war years. The Germans had built to last.

The small office and reception room near by looked freshly painted and from two white poles alongside it the flags of France and the United Kingdom were already flying.

Monsieur Pamplemousse wasn't sure whether the airship looked bigger or smaller than he'd expected. Both in a way. Close to and seen from below, the balloon itself looked vast – vast and slightly out of control; the gondola, with its large windows and helicopter-like Perspex dome surrounding the flight deck, like a pimple which had been added as an afterthought.

Two men in dark blue uniform came out of the office to greet him.

'Monsieur Pamplemousse?' The first one, grey-haired, with a weather-beaten face and an air of quiet authority, held out his hand to introduce himself. 'Commander Winters.' He turned and nodded to the second man. 'My colleague – Capitaine Leflaix of the French navy. I'm afraid,' he looked down at Pommes Frites, 'your dog will have to stay behind.'

'Stay behind?' repeated Monsieur Pamplemousse. 'Pommes Frites? But he always comes with me. Wherever we go.'

'Company orders, I'm afraid. *Chiens* are strictly *interdits*.' Clearly there was no point in arguing.

'*Là, là.*' Monsieur Pamplemousse bent down to give his friend and confidant a consoling pat. It struck him as he did so that Pommes Frites was taking the news of his deprivation remarkably well.

Looking round, he saw why. Some dozen or so of the waiting group had detached themselves from the main body and were clutching the gondola in an attempt to keep it steady ready for boarding. They weren't achieving one-hundred-per-cent success. The remaining men were clutching two bow lines like tug-of-war teams awaiting the signal for the off.

Commander Winters looked up at the sky. 'Right!' He clapped his hands briskly. 'We'll get you weighed first and then we'd better get cracking.' He led the way into the reception room and pointed to some scales. '*Parlez-vous anglais?'*

'Un petit peu,' said Monsieur Pamplemousse non-committally as he watched the needle shoot round. 'A little.'

Commander Winters looked at the scales. 'Aah!' He made the word sound like a black mark. Monsieur Pamplemousse wasn't sure if it referred to his lack of English or the figure on the dial; probably both. He followed the others back outside.

'You need always to face the airship,' said Capitaine Leflaix as he helped Monsieur Pamplemousse up a small flight of steps. 'Both getting in and getting out. Otherwise, it can take you by surprise.'

As Monsieur Pamplemousse missed the first step he saw what the other meant. Conscious of raised eyebrows and pained expressions on the faces of those trying to hold the gondola steady, he had another go, then paused momentarily in the doorway to wave *au revoir* to Pommes Frites. Pommes Frites wore his gloomy expression, as though 'goodbye – it's been nice knowing you' would have been more appropriate to the occasion. There was a clatter of feet from the other two as they followed him up the steps.

Monsieur Pamplemousse exchanged greetings with a girl in uniform as she moved forward to close the cabin door, then took stock of his surroundings. No expense had been spared for the forthcoming event. Everything smelled new. The floor was luxuriously carpeted in deep blue. There were eight spotlessly clean wine-red armchair-type seats, two at the far end of the cabin and four grouped around a small rosewood table aft of the open flight deck. Suddenly the scale of reference had changed again. Now that he could no longer see the balloon, the gondola felt unexpectedly spacious, like the sitting-room of a small flat – except, as far as he could see, there was no galley and no room to put one, only a door marked TOILETTES and what could have been a small cocktail cabinet; someone must have got their finger out already. All the same, he could see problems ahead. In the end prepared trays might be necessary – small ones at that! The Director would not be pleased.

Leflaix emerged from the flight deck carrying a small pair of portable steps. He mounted them, opened a domed porthole in the roof, and stretched up to peer through the gap.

Wondering irreverently if he was looking to see if they were still attached to the balloon or whether it had floated off without them, Monsieur Pamplemousse settled himself in one of the chairs by the table so that he would have somewhere to work and make notes.

Leflaix closed the hatch. 'I was checking the ballonet bags to make sure we are stabilised.' His expression was wry. 'You need to be a sailor as well as an airman to fly an airship.' He took his place on the flight deck.

The girl appeared and handed him a brochure. '*Monsieur* must be very important for the airship to fly on a day like today.'

Monsieur Pamplemousse gave a non-committal shrug. Nevertheless, he couldn't help feeling flattered.

He flipped through the pages. It was full of technical details: gross volume – 6,666 cubic metres, length – 59 metres, maximum speed – 60 knots, endurance – 24 hours, engines – two turbo-charged Porsche . . .

He had hardly finished reading the last few words when a seat belt warning light above the flight-deck bulkhead came on and there was a roar from somewhere behind him as first one and then the other of the two engines were started up. He looked through the window. The two large fans mounted towards the rear of the gondola had begun to turn.

As the crew completed their cockpit check, the men outside who had been holding the gondola steady began removing bags of ballast, while those holding the lines got ready to take the strain. He felt the pilot take control as the nose of the airship was detached from its mooring and the fans were rotated until they were at an angle of 45 degrees facing the ground.

Hand signals were exchanged and the airship began moving forward, slowly at first, then faster, until suddenly the ground started to slip away from them as the craft rose, nose down, into the air. He had a momentary feeling of guilt as he caught a glimpse of Pommes Frites. His mouth was open as though he was howling and his plaster was hanging loose. Then they turned to port and the concrete area disappeared from view.

Almost immediately they were over the cliffs, with the sea breaking angrily in clouds of white foam on the granite rocks below. It looked as though they were in for a spell of bad weather. The wind must be coming up from the Bay of Biscay.

He tried to break the ice with the stewardess. 'I think, *Mademoiselle*, we are better off up here, *n'est-ce pas?*'

She looked at him in surprise, as though the very idea was extraordinary, then disappeared behind some curtains at the rear of the compartment. Clearly she was in no mood for making polite conversation.

Monsieur Pamplemousse gave a shrug as the airship executed a wide turn to port, skirted along past St. Marc, where Monsieur Hulot spent his famous holiday, and headed for the Côte d'Amour around La Baule. He reached for his camera as he looked out of the window and saw people on the beach stand up to wave as they flew over. This was the life. There was no doubt about it – the Director was right – the dirigible was an elegant solution to the problem of manned flight. He ought to consider himself lucky to enjoy such a unique experience.

A moment later they had crossed the narrow strip of town and were over the Grande Brière, the vast area of swamp and marshland behind La Baule, home of peat-diggers and rush gatherers. Its streams were full of eels, pike, roach and wild-fowl, their banks yellow with iris in spring and early summer.

Monsieur Pamplemousse began to wish he'd brought more film; his automatic winder had been working overtime. By the time they headed west towards the sea he could hardly have documented the area more fully had he been commissioned to make an aerial survey.

To his left he could see a group of islands; ahead of them

was the long arm of the Quiberon peninsula. The few people out and about hardly bothered to look up as they passed over. Most of them seemed too busy packing up their belongings. A *vedette* scuttled across the bay, heading towards the harbour.

Monsieur Pamplemousse was so busy with his camera he was scarcely aware of the motion, which was not unpleasant at first – a little like drifting at sea in a small boat, rising and falling with the waves. If every so often the Captain pushed the nose down in order to pin-point a landmark, so much the better; it gave him a better angle, as did the rolling gently first to one side and then the other. He managed to get a particularly good shot of the oyster-beds in Locmariaquer from a near vertical position. And when the nose went in the opposite direction – towards the sky – it gave him a chance to reload. He wished now he had brought his entire range of lenses and filters. Some of the cloud effects could have been quite spectacular through a dark filter; one moment black and angry-looking, the next moment like an etching as the sun broke through a gap and make a bright rim round their edge.

He could now see why so many postcards on sale in the local shops were shots taken from the air. Seen from ground level much of the countryside was flat and uninteresting; from some three or four hundred metres up, the Golfe du Morbihan was a wonderful series of creeks and inlets and the land behind it a maze-like pattern of fields and stone walls. With a bit of luck he would have enough pictures to warrant a whole series of articles in *L'Escargot – Le Guide*'s staff magazine.

At first Leflaix came to see him from time to time, but gradually his visits became less frequent. He seemed more interested in the stewardess, who had joined the others on the flight-deck, peering over their shoulders at the view ahead.

Carnac appeared on the starboard side, coinciding with a break in the clouds. The sudden burst of sunshine made the rows of menhirs look like lines of Roman soldiers forming up to do battle. As they flew over, the shadow cast by the airship seemed strange, almost threatening.

Having decided to save the rest of his film for the return journey, Monsieur Pamplemousse settled down at the table. Things had gone quiet in the cabin and it was time to start work.

Feeling inside his jacket he removed a long white envelope which bore, on the back flap, an embossed reproduction of *Le Guide*'s symbol – two crossed *escargots* rampant. It contained the letter the Director had given him before he left, outlining his own plans for the inaugural flight.

Knowing how long-winded the Director could be when he got his hands on a dictating machine, Monsieur Pamplemousse had put off reading it for as long as possible. The Director was inclined to write as he spoke; brevity was not his strong point.

He skipped the first two pages, which were mostly a repeat of all that had been said in his office the day before. It read as though he had been interrupted in mid-sentence by the telephone, not once, but several times. It wasn't until the middle of page three that he got to the heart of the matter.

'. . . in short, Pamplemousse, my suggestion, and it *is* only a suggestion, but a good one, I think, nonetheless, is that we should confine ourselves to no more than six courses; simple peasant dishes of the kind one might find in any little café or bistro in the area over which the dirigible will be flying. Dishes that reveal the true glory of France – its food. If there is sufficient time, we might even produce a special souvenir *carte* on the cover of which, inscribed in gold leaf, are those very words: *Les Six Gloires de la France.* Underneath one could add the symbol of *Le Guide*; two *escargots* rampant. There is no reason why we should not profit from the occasion.

'Now, to start with, one might have some of those little pastry delicacies – their correct name escapes me – but they are stuffed with *foie gras* and served alongside raw oysters. The two go particularly well together, especially when accompanied by a glass of very cold Château d'Yquem – I would suggest the '66. You may if you wish, leave that to me. I have a particularly good source.

'After that, how about some *Oeufs Pochés aux Moules*? Eggs poached in the juice in which some mussels have been cooked. I had it the other evening. The eggs and the mussels should be served with *Hollandaise* sauce. I am told that for the dish to be at its best the eggs should be as fresh as possible . . .'

Suddenly aware that a gust of wind was blowing them sideways, Monsieur Pamplemousse looked out of the window. They were now flying inland. It was hard to make out where they were. He peered at the scene through his binoculars and immediately wished he hadn't. All he could see was endless fields of artichokes. They looked rather sad, as though they, too, felt they had seen the best of the day. He wondered when the Director had last eaten in a simple Breton bistro. The menu might also account for his being on a diet; a sad state of affairs for the editor of the most prestigious of France's many food guides. It sounded as though he was mentally trying to make up for lost meals.

'. . . lobster, of course – or a *Langouste* – perhaps *à la crème*, followed by a roast duck from Nantes. As I am sure you know, it is at its best when cooked in a sauce made from butter, cream and *eau-de-vie de Muscadet*. I will leave the choice of wine to you.

'By that time they should be over Normandy where cream really comes into its own. I believe *les Anglais* often prefer to have their cheese at the end of a meal – a habit they most certainly didn't acquire from the Normans. However, ours is not to reason why. That being so, we could continue the theme of simplicity with some of those delicious tartlets made with eggs and almonds and cream which are a speciality of the area. I believe they are known as *Mirlitons* . . .'

Monsieur Pamplemousse had some difficulty focusing on the next page as the airship hit a pocket of air and fell rapidly before rising, nose-up again. Out of the corner of his eye he saw the hostess buckling herself into a seat. He thought she looked rather white.

'. . . then, Pamplemousse . . .' Monsieur Pamplemousse could almost sense from the writing – the way the letters were slanted, that the Director was about to produce one of his masterstrokes, '. . . then, Camembert should be served – preferably a non-pasteurised example from the Pays d'Ange. Although the season is almost over, I have a special reason for suggesting it rather than, say, a Pont-l'Evêque or a Brillat-Savarin. Legend has it that when Napoleon first tasted Camembert he kissed the waitress who had the honour of serving him. So, who knows? With the exercise of a little tact, one might arrange matters . . .

'Once again, Pamplemousse, I leave it to your good judgement. You have so much more experience in these affairs than I.

'To round things off, for by that time they should be on the last leg of their epic journey and nearing *Londres*, in deference to our English guests, I suggest that with the *café* we serve, instead of *petits fours*, one of their own specialities. There is one I am thinking of which they call "trifle". I have looked it up in one of their recipe books – a slim volume – it was left behind by an English girl we had staying with us a few years ago. You may remember her – a blonde girl with a predilection for a dish called "Spotted Dick". For some reason my wife took a dislike to her and she had to go, but she was something of an expert on what the English call "puddings". I believe that before she left England for France she had been a member of a well-known pudding club.'

Monsieur Pamplemousse closed his eyes. He did indeed remember the Director's *au pair*. Elsie had been her name. An unusually well-endowed girl, she had given a whole new meaning to the words '*au pair*'. He wasn't in the slightest bit surprised she had been told to leave. Puddings were probably not the only thing she was expert at.

'It seems to be a concoction which is made by emptying the contents of a can of tinned fruit over what are known as "sponge-fingers", which have themselves been previously steeped in sherry. The whole is then immersed in something they call "bird's custard". I cannot imagine what that is, nor what it tastes like – I have enquired at *Fauchon* and they have promised to telephone me back, but they have yet to do so – however, it appears to be very popular. The dish is then topped by a layer of thick cream . . .

'I am not sure what would go with it; the combination might prove altogether too rich, but if there is any of the Château d'Yquem left –'

The airship gave a lurch. Monsieur Pamplemousse suddenly felt extremely sick. Several things were abundantly clear. Not only was the Director sadly out of touch with the eating habits of both the English and the peasants of Brittany, he had never been up in a balloon either. Speaking for himself, he had never felt less like eating in his life. The *crêpe* he'd consumed at breakfast had been a ghastly mistake; the *croissants* a cardinal error; as for the *chocolat* . . .

Regardless of the sign warning him to keep his seat-belt fastened, Monsieur Pamplemousse released the clip and staggered towards the rear of the airship. He beat the stewardess by a short head, but he pretended not to have seen her. Never had the word TOILETTES looked so welcoming, nor a basin coming up to greet him so inviting. Pushing the door shut behind him with his foot, he slid the catch home all in one movement. It was no time for old-fashioned gallantry, more a case of every *homme* for himself. Not the most engaging girl he had ever met. No doubt she was prone to headaches.

Like the sign on the bulkhead above the flight-deck, the word OCCUPÉ above the toilet door stayed illuminated for the rest of the flight. Monsieur Pamplemousse was not in a mood to receive other callers. His head was spinning. His stomach ached – it felt as though it had been wrenched out at the roots. He was alternately bathed in sweat and shivering with cold. He hadn't felt quite so ill since the time just after the war when he'd crossed *La Manche* during mid-winter on a visit to England. Death would have come as a welcome relief. He wasn't even aware they had landed until he heard a familiar scratching noise on the other side of the door and realised that the engines had been turned off.

Pommes Frites' relief at his master's safe return was tempered with an understanding that all was not well. His welcome was suitably muted. In any case he seemed to have other things on his mind. Once he'd exchanged greetings and bestowed a welcoming lick, he disappeared outside again. There was a thoughtful expression on his face which, under normal circumstances, his master would have registered immediately and wondered at. As it was, Monsieur Pamplemousse still had problems of his own.

He began gathering up his belongings, some of which had fallen to the floor. Fortunately that didn't include the Leica, which was still on the table where he had left it. The stewardess was nowhere to be seen. She must have beaten Pommes Frites to the steps.

'Sorry about that.' Commander Winters climbed out of his seat. 'We wouldn't normally have gone up on a day like today, but your boss was most insistent when I telephoned him this morning to try and call it off. He said it was absolute top priority. Nothing must stop us. I hope you got what you wanted.'

Monsieur Pamplemousse had a mental picture of the Director sitting in his office, totally oblivious to the plight of others. He made a mental note to get his own back one day should the opportunity arise.

'Er, I wonder if you'd mind doing something about your dog? I think he is about to attack one of our chaps.'

Monsieur Pamplemousse joined Commander Winters at the cabin door and was staggered to see Pommes Frites at the foot of the steps, fangs bared, apparently engaged in a tug-of-war with one of the ground staff over a bag of ballast. The man appeared petrified, as well he might in the circumstances. When he felt like it, Pommes Frites could look extremely menacing. His plaster had disappeared and he was positively quivering with excitement as he dug his paws into the ground, absolutely refusing to let go of his end. The accompanying

70

sound effects boded ill for anyone rash enough to try and thwart him.

'*Sacrebleu!*' Monsieur Pamplemousse clambered down the steps as fast as he could go. '*Asseyez-vous!*' The command, rapped out with all the authority he could muster, had an immediate effect.

Looking suitably ashamed, Pommes Frites let go of his end and sat to attention. If a flicker of surprise entered his eyes that his master should take the other man's part, it was only momentary. He was too well trained to protest out loud.

'Never mind. I expect he's glad to see you back.' Commander Winters stifled Monsieur Pamplemousse's apologies. 'Who's a good boy, then?' He bent down to pat Pommes Frites and then thought better of it. Instead, he picked up the bag. 'Perhaps you'd like to keep this as a souvenir?'

'*Merci* – you are very kind.' Monsieur Pamplemousse would have been hard put to think of anything he wanted less as a souvenir than a ten kilogram bag of ballast. He tried to look suitably grateful as he took it, but he could see why the Commander had made the gesture. It was wet from Pommes Frites' saliva.

Leflaix clattered down the steps, his expression grieved. Perhaps he felt disappointed at having been let down by a fellow-countryman.

'You should always face the airship as you leave,' he reminded Pamplemousse stiffly. 'Otherwise it may take you by surprise.'

Monsieur Pamplemousse looked at his watch. It was midday. They had been up for less than an hour, but it could have been ten times as long. The last twenty minutes had seemed like forever. He said goodbye to the others and made his way unsteadily towards his car.

Throwing the bag in the back of the car, he started the engine and drove off.

'Don't forget to face the airship!' The words were permanently engraved on Monsieur Pamplemousse's mind as he acknowledged the salute from the man on duty at the gate and headed back towards Port St. Augustin. At that moment in time he felt as though he never wanted to look an airship in the face again. All he wanted to do was lie down somewhere and rest. But the grass at the side of the road looked damp and uninviting and the prospect of going back to the Ty Coz was not a happy one.

After a kilometre or so he opened the window to let in a welcome draught of cold air and almost at once started to feel better. He wondered if he should try his luck at the Hôtel du Port. A *digestif* of some kind might help, and if that did the trick, in the fullness of time he might even attempt an omelette; plain, of course, but with a *salade de tomates* and a slice or two of *baguette*. After that, he could explore the possibility of their having a room vacant. Whoever said 'man cannot think on an empty stomach' had a point. One way and another he had a lot to brood over.

Monsieur Pamplemousse wasn't the only one with things on his mind. Pommes Frites had remained unusually quiet during the journey, putting two and two together, first one way and then another, and each time coming up with another answer. His schooling had been based on the computer-like principle that black is black and white is white. The possibility of there being various shades of grey in between had not been introduced to his curriculum in case it led to confusion. Besides, he knew what he knew. The fact that his master didn't seem at all interested in knowing about it, he put down to a temporary lapse brought on, not unsurprisingly in his view, by the previous evening's meal followed by going up in a balloon. A lethal combination.

What, in Pommes Frites' humble opinion, his master needed most in order to restore him to good health was some grass. In fact, he fully expected him to pull in to the side of the road at any moment so that he could gather some.

Pommes Frites' training was also based on a system which recognised good work when it saw it and rewarded it accordingly – usually with a suitable tit-bit from the *boucherie*. So far that reward had not been forthcoming. Neither, for that matter, had there been much in the way of recompense for the unwarranted attack on his nose.

It was with these thoughts uppermost in his mind that he followed his master into the bar of the Hôtel du Port, and shortly afterwards outside again onto the terrace.

The bad weather had driven most of the people off the beach and into the cafés, restaurants and *crêperies* around the harbour. Monsieur Pamplemousse had to squeeze his way through a maze of beach-bags, sunshades and other impedimenta to reach the one remaining table in the corner nearest the sea. A smell of damp clothes filled the air. He felt sorry for all those who'd been looking forward to a sun-drenched holiday; even more sorry for the waitresses who were struggling to serve them.

Corks popped, plates clattered. Orders shouted over the heads of the diners were repeated by a disembodied voice from somewhere inside the hotel. Cries of '*un Muscadet*' echoed from all sides, and were repeated as bottles were plunged into buckets of ice.

He wondered if any of the old staff were still there. Most of them had probably got married by now, or forsaken Brittany for the promise of a better life in Paris. The fourteenth *arrondissement* was full of girls who had left home in search of fame and fortune but who had got no further than the area around the Gare Montparnasse. The girl who took his order looked as though she would have happily settled for that with no questions asked. Her *coiffe* was not at its best, her matching lace apron looked decidedly ruffled.

A large and juicy steak was deposited on a nearby serving table by another waitress while she went off for the rest of her order. Monsieur Pamplemousse studiously averted his gaze. Steak was not what he fancied most at that moment. Despite his musings the night before, it was not high on his list of choices when he was staying in an area noted for its seafood, and in his present state of health it had very low priority indeed.

However, at that moment there occurred a strange and

unexpected diversion which totally took his mind off his surroundings and made even Pommes Frites sit up and take notice.

Making her way slowly along the deserted promenade there appeared an elderly female of such bizarre appearance it almost took the breath away. The whole restaurant went quiet at the same instant. One moment it had been all noise and chatter, the next moment silence descended as everybody stopped eating and turned to watch her progress towards them.

In his time, when mingling among the down-and-outs under the bridges of the Seine had been all part of a night's work, Monsieur Pamplemousse thought he had seen everything. But even the bell which once upon a time rang at the old *Les Halles* vegetable market, signalling the end of trading for the day and the moment when the *clochards* could take their pick of the leftovers, had never brought forth such a truly wretched specimen of humanity.

Two nuns came round a corner, crossed themselves, and then disappeared back the way they had come. A gendarme suddenly discovered he was needed urgently elsewhere and followed suit.

As she loomed nearer, the old woman looked, if possible, even more malodorous. Her putty-coloured hair hung in great knots down her back. The several layers of cardigan covering her upper half were topped by a scarf so matted it looked as though it must have been glued in place. Her feet, partially encased in a pair of ancient carpet slippers held together by string, were black with the dirt of ages. A slit up one side of a grey skirt revealed the top of an even greyer stocking held in place by yet another piece of string. String, in fact, seemed to play an important part in the old woman's attire. It looked as though anyone foolish enough – or drunk enough – to pull one of the ends would have caused the whole ensemble to collapse.

Much to Monsieur Pamplemousse's dismay she came to a halt almost directly opposite his table. Waving a battered parasol with one hand and brandishing an empty wine bottle above her head with the other, she began screaming in a shrill voice for the patron.

Monsieur Pamplemousse eyed her uneasily, uncomfortably aware that his was the only table on the terrace with a spare seat. The possibility of sharing a meal with such an object was not a happy one. He prayed that his omelette wouldn't arrive. It had been a mistake to ask for it *baveuse*; it could be as overdone as they liked. It could be left to cook for another ten minutes if need be.

He did his best to avoid the old crone's gaze as she swayed closer and closer, leaning back in his chair as she thrust the empty wine bottle in his face.

Fortunately, he was saved the ultimate embarrassment by the arrival of the *Madame*. She was closely followed by the chef brandishing a large kitchen knife.

His presence was unnecessary. *Madame* was quite capable of dealing with the situation; her vocabulary was more than equal to the task. No conceivable occupation, no possible country of origin was omitted from the list of permutations she flung at the unwelcome intruder. Her performance drew a round of applause.

Pursued by cries of '*vieille toupie, vieille bique, boche, rastaquouère*', pausing only to indulge herself in the luxury of that classic gesture of contempt – '*le bras d'honneur*' the slapping of the right arm above the elbow by the palm of the left, causing the former to rise sharply upwards, the old woman disappeared along the promenade rather faster than she arrived.

'*Pardon, Monsieur. Poof! L'alcoolo!*' The *Madame* squeezed her way past.

Monsieur Pamplemousse offered his thanks, then bent down and reached under the table. In her haste to leave, the old crone had dropped her bottle. He looked at it thoughtfully, then raised it to his nose and cautiously sniffed the opening. It smelled of honeysuckle.

He wondered. The bottle was empty, but according to the

label it had once contained wine from Savennières, an area just to the north of Angers; a Coulée de Serrant at that – something of a rarity. Not the usual tipple of a wino. And if the lingering bouquet was anything to go by, it had been opened quite recently.

There was something else that bothered him. The old woman had been close enough for him to have caught the full force of any bodily odours she might have had. Expecting the worst – the nauseating, overpoweringly sweet smell which only the extremely unwashed manage to achieve – he'd instinctively drawn himself back. But it hadn't been like that at all. What little scent he'd detected had really been quite pleasant; more male oriented than female. He was no great expert, but if he'd been asked he would have said it was that of a fairly expensive after-shave.

Hearing a commotion going on behind him, Monsieur Pamplemousse turned in his seat. It didn't need any great powers of detection to see what had happened and to arrive at an immediate solution. While everyone's attention had been focused on the goings-on with the old woman, someone had helped themselves to the steak.

In looking for the culprit, the one advantage he had over the others was that he could see Pommes Frites under the table and they couldn't. Pommes Frites had his eyes closed, but his face said it all. It could have been summed up in the one word – *extase*. And if concrete rather than circumstantial evidence were called for, salivary tests would have been money down the drain. His lips were covered in meat juice. Others may have abandoned their cutlery, but it took a lot to put Pommes Frites off his food.

Monsieur Pamplemousse called for the bill. On the pretext of feeling unwell he paid it as soon as it came and left without waiting for the change. It was only a matter of time before those around him realised what had happened, and when they did, one thing was very certain, it would not be an ideal moment to broach the subject of a room for the night.

He had left the car in a space a little way along the front, and as he walked towards it felt in a quandary. He could hardly punish Pommes Frites in front of all the people in the Hôtel. It would give the game away.

On the other hand, as with a small child, punishment needed to be carried out immediately – otherwise it would be extremely unfair. Pommes Frites would think it was yet another unprovoked assault and he would be most unhappy.

That was another thing. Far from looking repentant, Pommes Frites' behaviour was entirely the opposite. Goodness as well as repleteness shone from his eyes. A halo would not have looked out of place; one of the larger sizes. He looked for all the world like a bloodhound who felt himself in line for a medal for services rendered.

Monsieur Pamplemousse was still puzzling over what to do for the best when they reached the car. He let Pommes Frites into the back and was about to climb in himself when he paused and looked across the road, hardly able to believe what he saw.

It was the old woman again. She was skulking behind the *Sanisette*. Worse still, she was clearly beckoning to him. Even as he watched she lifted up her skirt suggestively and started performing a jig. It was not a pretty sight. With the total dedication of a Cartier-Bresson and throwing caution to the winds, Monsieur Pamplemousse pointed his camera in her direction and once again used up the rest of his film. Fortunately, he had left the motor wind on his camera. At least it was all over quickly.

Slamming the 2CV into gear, Monsieur Pamplemousse manoeuvred it out of the parking space. The thought uppermost in his mind was to put as much distance between himself and Port St. Augustin as he could in the fastest possible time.

At the roundabout opposite the *Mairie* he took the road signposted to Nantes. If he did nothing else that afternoon, at least he could dispatch his films to Headquarters. If he was in time to put them on an afternoon train, Trigaux in the art department would have them first thing in the morning. With luck, they would be processed and on their way back to him by the end of the day.

After that he might call in at a local *vétérinaire*. Pommes Frites' behaviour had really been most peculiar. It was quite out of character, and totally against his past training. To behave badly once was forgivable, but twice in one morning was not. Either the wound in his nose was troubling him – it could be that there was something in the ink – or there was another, less obvious, cause. Whatever the reason, it definitely needed looking into.

And after that . . . after that he would stop at a *fleuriste* and buy some flowers for the girl. He could call in with them later that afternoon.

It was early evening before Monsieur Pamplemousse finally got back to the hotel. He parked his car unobtrusively between two British cars, an elderly Rover and a Bentley, and unpacked his luggage.

The news of Yasmin was not good. She had been sent to a larger hospital in Nantes where they had more specialist treatment. He could have kicked himself for not telephoning first, for he must have passed within half a kilometre of her while he was there. At least the flowers were being sent on.

The doctor at the local hospital had been very cagey and full of questions.

'Did she drink?'

'Was she addicted to drugs?'

The answer to all of them was he didn't know. Given her occupation, it seemed unlikely.

'No, there was no point in going to see her. She wasn't allowed visitors.' It was all very depressing.

He had hoped to creep back up to his room unnoticed, but the owner of the Ty Coz was behind the reception desk.

'*Monsieur* is back!'

'*Oui.*' He tried to make it sound as though he had never intended leaving.

The owner looked at his cases. 'We had thought . . .'

'I had need of them,' said Monsieur Pamplemousse simply.

'Ah!'

'Now, if you will excuse me . . .'

'*Un moment, Monsieur*. There is a letter for you. It came during *dîner* last night, but you had already retired to your room. I would have given it to you this morning with your *petit déjeuner*, but . . .' Monsieur Pamplemousse was left in no doubt as to where the fault lay.

The envelope was plain. On the outside it said simply 'Monsieur Pamplemousse, Ty Coz'. He didn't recognise the writing.

'There was no other message?' He slid his thumb under the flap and removed a single sheet of white paper.

'*Non, Monsieur*. It must have been delivered by hand while everyone was busy in the restaurant. It was found on the desk.'

He read the note several times. It was brief and to the point: the salient words were heavily underlined.

'I *must see you*. Please *do not come to me. I* will come to *you*, later tonight after the show. Take *great care!*'

It was signed Yasmin.

His mind in a whirl, Monsieur Pamplemousse slipped the note back into its envelope. If only he'd taken the bull by the horns and gone to the circus the night before . . . But he hadn't, so there was no point in wishing he had. All the same, he couldn't rid his mind of Madame Caoutchouc's parting words – the one word the girl had repeated over and over again as she was taken away.

He suddenly realised the owner was talking to him. '*Pardon.*'

'*Monsieur* will be wanting *dîner* tonight?'

'*Non*.' He folded the letter and slipped it into an inside pocket. '*Non, merci.*

'Pommes Frites and I are going to the circus. I doubt if we shall be back until late.'

5

A Touch of Pneumatics

Madame Caoutchouc had been wrong in prophesying that no one would be going to the circus. Monsieur Pamplemousse found himself at the tail end of a long queue and spent the next fifteen minutes shuffling along at a snail's pace while he reflected on the strange make-up of human beings. Tragedy acted like a magnet. In the past he'd known people drive for miles in order to visit the scene of a particularly gruesome murder, often bringing the entire family with them so that they could make a day of it. Listening to some of the conversations going on around him it was obvious many of those present were enjoying a vicarious pleasure in discussing the gory details. Everyone had their theories. Overnight, people who had probably never done anything more adventurous than stand on the seat of a garden swing had become experts on the trapeze. He chose not to listen. Half of them wouldn't have been there normally. One couple had travelled all the way from Rennes, nearly one hundred and fifty kilometres away. He wondered what Yasmin herself would have thought had she known.

The noise was deafening. The side shows in the Fair were doing a roaring trade. Overall there was a strange acrid-sweet smell, a mixture of candy-floss, greasy frankfurters, and smoke from a *crêperie*. He was glad they had stopped for a bite to eat in St. Nazaire on the way back, otherwise he would have felt ravenous and he might have been tempted. His liver would have suffered. As it was, once he'd got his ticket he gladly made his escape from the crowd and joined Pommes Frites in the car while he waited for nine o'clock.

A clown on stilts passed by on the other side of the road, drumming up custom; hardly necessary in the circumstances, but it was probably part of a set routine. A small group of children followed on behind, shouting words of encouragement. One, braver than the rest, tried to push him over and received a clip around the back-side from a walking-stick for his pains. A cheer went up. Loud speakers outside the Big Top blared forth unintelligible announcements at intervals. He heard the sound of a lion roaring, but in the general hubbub it was hard to tell whether it was the real thing or simply a recording. If he could judge by what he had seen that morning, he strongly suspected the latter.

He glanced round. Oblivious to it all, Pommes Frites was fast asleep on the back seat next to his bag of ballast. Opening the glove compartment, Monsieur Pamplemousse took out a pocket torch and shone it on his watch. It showed five minutes to nine. There was still time enough to stroll round the outside of the circus before taking his seat. If past experience with travelling circuses was anything to go by it was unlikely to start on time. Probably most of those running the side-shows were involved in one way or another and would need to make a quick change.

He was right. By the time he reached the Fair half the stalls already had their shutters up and the rest were following suit. Nearly all the crowd had disappeared. The only noise came from a giant electric generator parked near the *carrousel*. There was an air of suppressed excitement overall. Madame Caoutchouc, looking darkly voluptuous, came out of her caravan wearing a patterned dressing-gown over her costume. As she reached the tent belonging to the smallest man in the world, she paused and called out. A moment later she was joined by a midget dressed as a clown, and together they

81

made their way towards the Big Top.

Monsieur Pamplemousse wondered whether to follow on behind, then he decided to explore the waste area near the back of the circus one more time. He had no idea what he was looking for, let alone where to start, but the sight of the girl's car still parked in the same place reminded him of the need to do something, however trivial-seeming.

He glanced around. There was an element missing, but he couldn't for the moment think what it could be. The BMW was in exactly the same place, alongside the generator lorry, but the blue van had been moved further away. He shone his torch on the tail-board. There were patches of mud which he hadn't registered earlier in the day. They looked fresh. The thin splashes had dried hard, but thick areas were still damp, and dark in colour. The rear wheels were covered with mud as well and there were bits of grass sticking to the walls of the tyres. He knelt down and felt the ground. There were marks which looked as though something heavy had been dragged along the surface.

Monsieur Pamplemousse was about to check the front of the van when he felt rather than saw a light go out in a nearby caravan. Switching off the torch, he backed into the shadows and waited. There was the whine of an electric motor, followed by the sound of a door being opened and shut. It was followed by the metallic click of a key being turned in a lock. The whole process was repeated. Then footsteps muffled by the grass passed him heading for the back of the tent. Whoever it was seemed to be in a hurry.

Taking a chance, Monsieur Pamplemousse peered round the side of the van and had a clear back view of a man in a dark cloak silhouetted against the light from the circus. A hood was pulled up over his head.

At that moment the muffled strains of martial music filled the air; 'The Grand March' from *Aida* played on drums and fifes, with a solitary trumpet in support by the sound of it. What it lacked in grandeur was more than made up for by sheer vigour, and any imperfections were drowned beneath the cheers from the audience.

He allowed a few seconds to pass and then made his way towards the entrance, subconsciously matching his pace to the time of the music. With luck he would catch the end of the Grand Parade and a front view of the man he'd just seen. If anyone had asked why it seemed important, he couldn't have answered.

In the event he was fortunate to get a seat. All the rows near the front were jam-packed, and he only just managed to squeeze onto the end of a bench near the back.

He recognised the man instantly even without his cloak. He had an air about him, as though he was at one and the same time both part of and yet separate from the whole. It was clear from the way he walked and the slightly arrogant look on his face as he led the parade out of the ring that he considered himself the star of the show. Perhaps he had usurped Yasmin's place. The last time Monsieur Pample- mousse had seen him he'd been behind the wheel of the van which had followed the girl into town.

Once again, Monsieur Pamplemousse had the feeling of having seen him somewhere before, some echo from the dim and distant past. Either that or a picture of him. He wasn't often wrong about such things. It was annoying because conundrums of this sort were liable to keep him awake at night, and he had lost enough sleep already.

He also recognised the man he'd spoken to outside the ticket office earlier in the day – now resplendent in the red frock-coat of a ring-master. He was introducing 'Madame Caoutchouc' in a 'death-defying act' – wrestling with a crocodile.

While the man did his build-up, Monsieur Pamplemousse took stock of his surroundings. It was a long time since he had been to a circus. Once upon a time, when he was a boy, it had been nearly all animal acts – lions, tigers, elephants, performing dogs and bears; now acrobats and jugglers were back in fashion.

Unusually for a small travelling circus, the king-poles were made of steel. Perhaps that was another sign of the changing times. It was logical. As well as being safer in a strong wind, steel poles would have allowed the height of the roof to be raised and with it the height of the trapeze. All the same the girl must have fallen many times before. Perhaps it was a case of one time too many. It happened; people injured themselves every day falling off step ladders or doing something equally mundane like tripping over a broken paving stone.

He applauded mechanically as the band reached a crescendo and the lights dimmed, only to be replaced by the flickering of a stroboscopic spot lamp as Madame Caoutchouc dashed into the ring clutching a fully-grown crocodile in her arms. She landed in the sawdust with the beast on top of her and for a moment or two it was hard to tell which way the struggle was going as they rolled around – a mass of threshing arms and legs. At first the flickering light seemed an unnecessary embellishment, but gradually it had a mesmerising effect. It was like watching a rapidly changing series of old-fashioned still pictures. First the crocodile was on top, then Madame Caoutchouc, then the crocodile again. Their positions changed almost faster than the eye or the brain could cope with. Finally, as the music reached a climax, Madame Caoutchouc managed to kneel astride the animal. Clasping it around the middle she gradually lifted it off the ground, centimetre by centimetre, until they were both upright. The tent went quiet as the crocodile thrashed to and fro, finally giving her a blow with its tail which would have floored most of those watching.

Monsieur Pamplemousse joined in the applause as Madame Caoutchouc at long last managed to extricate herself from the crocodile's grip, then forced its jaws open and placed her head inside its open mouth. Sooner her than him. The things some people did for a living; twice daily at that!

As she staggered from the ring, breathing heavily, the lights came up and the audience relaxed. A midget and another clown – an *Auguste*, the one with the red nose who always gets the custard pie – ran on and went through the age-old routine of balancing a bucket of water on the end of a pole. The shrieks as it fell off, threatening to soak those in the front row before they realised it was empty, were equalled only by the gales of laughter when a full bucket of water landed on the second clown. The rickety tiers supporting the audience swayed in sympathy. There was no gag like an old gag.

Half of him wondered if he should take the girl's note to the local police, but that would only involve a lot of tedious explanations. More than likely someone there would recognise him. They would want to know why he was in Port St. Augustin in the first place – by himself at that. It would all take up a lot more time than he could afford. The Director would not be pleased. The temptation to do a bit of ground work first was hard to resist. Afterwards he could decide on what action to take.

The clowns dashed off and were replaced by a girl doing handstands on the legs of an upturned table. The same girl repeated the trick to greater effect shortly afterwards on the back of one of the Arab ponies. Was she, he wondered, being groomed as a second Yasmin? She looked like a younger sister. Moments after her act was finished she joined the small band above the entrance to the ring, adding fife-playing to her other talents.

Madame Caoutchouc reappeared as the 'Indiarubber Lady', distracting attention while a cage was erected by tying herself up in knots to the tune of 'Over the Waves', whilst at the same time making a cup of coffee.

She could have saved herself the trouble. The act which followed was something of an anti-climax. Neither the lion nor its temporary keeper made any pretence at going near each other. Perhaps they both suffered from bad breath.

Monsieur Pamplemousse found his attention wandering. Clearly it was a case of 'the show must go on', but it was a struggle. The barrel was being well and truly scraped and there was a feeling of sadness about it all.

He kept his seat during the interval, feeling that if he once got up he might not return. He wondered what on earth he was doing here anyway. Was it just the romantic notion of it all? Had he temporarily seen himself as d'Artagnan rescuing a damsel in distress? The combination of a pretty girl and the age-old lure of the circus. He corrected himself. The combination of a pretty girl, the lure of the circus and a desperate note. It was a case of locking the stable door after the horse had bolted, but he had to start somewhere.

There was something else that bothered him about the note. He took it out and read it again, even though he knew it by heart. It wasn't simply a plea for help, there was an underlying message in it for him as well. 'Take *great care*.' The last two words were even more heavily underlined than the earlier ones.

'I *must see you*. Please *do not come to me. I* will come to *you*, later tonight after the show. Take *great care*!'

It was almost as though she had wanted to tell him something, the knowledge of which would put him in some kind of danger too.

But there had been no 'after the show'. In fact, the more he thought about it the more convinced he became that Yasmin's fall had been no accident. It was too much of a coincidence. Perhaps she had been wrought up over something, perhaps it *had* been a momentary lack of concentration on her part. But even that didn't ring true. In his experience, when it came to the crunch, people working in jobs requiring total concentration were capable of switching off to everything else, including personal problems.

He wondered about the man he'd seen driving the van. He seemed to be the odd one out. 'The Great Christoph' was how he'd been billed when he'd done a brief 'strong-man' act halfway though the first half. Apart from that one appearance he'd neither played in the band nor shown his face since the opening parade.

The answer came towards the end of the second half of the programme and left him with a strange mixture of feelings. The newspaper report had made no mention of Yasmin having a partner and from the artist's impression on the poster he had assumed she was a solo act; it had really been a case of the eye reading what the brain expected it to see. It hadn't crossed his mind that the man had also been part of her act.

A hush fell over the audience as the lights over the ring were dimmed and Christoph entered the ring and began climbing a rope hanging against one of the king-poles. It was the moment most of them had been waiting for.

No wonder the man had been keeping a low profile. It was hard to picture how he must be feeling at this moment, particularly if the accident had been the result of a row. There was no doubt in Monsieur Pamplemousse's mind that for whatever reason the girl had been avoiding her partner. Avoiding him, or . . . avoiding him seeing her with anyone else.

He concentrated on the figure of Christoph as he reached a platform near the roof of the tent on the far side of the ring. Stripped to the waist, the gold cross dangling from his neck, he posed for a second or two while he regained his breath. Taking advantage of the moment, Monsieur Pamplemousse picked up his camera and zoomed in to as tight a shot as possible. The single spotlight produced a halo effect making it difficult to focus.

Perhaps it was a simple case of jealousy. Greeks were renowned for it, guarding what they considered to be their property even unto death.

He pressed the shutter six times, then Christoph made a gesture towards the ring. Another spotlight came on and a murmur went round the audience as it revealed the young girl standing at the foot of the opposite pole. It was followed almost immediately by a burst of applause as she took a quick bow and then began her climb, moving with lightness and ease, hand over hand, towards the top.

There was a low drum-roll as she unhitched a pole suspended from the roof by two ropes. It grew louder and louder as she climbed on and began to swing backwards and forwards towards her partner. There was a gasp from the audience, first of horror, then of relief as she appeared to slip and caught her heels on the pole at the very last moment, so that she was hanging upside down.

There was no doubt about it, they were both milking the situation for all it was worth. And why not? She deserved every ounce of applause for her courage. He glanced down at the ring. A group of men were standing round the safety-net. Their faces showed clearly the anxiety they felt as they followed her every movement to and fro.

Monsieur Pamplemousse slipped quietly from his seat and made his way out of the tent. It wasn't squeamishness. He simply wanted time to think, and he doubted very much if lightning would strike twice in the same place.

Outside the air was cool. There was a full moon and the sky was crowded with stars. The immediate area was totally deserted. Everyone must be inside watching the act. Another loud drum-roll sounded, followed by a burst of applause.

Almost without thinking he made his way back towards the caravan. Quite possibly, if Yasmin and the Great Christoph had formed themselves into an act, they also lived together. They might even be married. Literally putting your life in someone else's hands day in, day out, pre-supposed a closer than average relationship. But if that was the case, why had Yasmin sent the note? He still couldn't rid himself of the uneasy feeling that it had to do with something she had wished to keep from her partner.

The caravan was an American Barth. That accounted for the whine he had heard which would have come from the electrically operated steps. Even from the outside it looked as if it had everything and it probably did. A state-of-the-art multi-purpose aerial on the roof summed it all up. Again, why not? Travelling fairs and circuses were always an odd mixture of the tawdry and the up-to-date. Showmen were renowned for their caravans. It was where all the money went; an outward sign of success. The second lock on the door was a recent addition. It was French; a Vachette double cylinder multilock. Anyone breaking in would find it easier to cut a hole in the side of the caravan. There was mud on the steps, the same colour as that on the back of the blue van.

The blinds were lowered on all the side windows. Tinted glass around the driving compartment made it impossible to see inside.

Near the main door stood a portable waste-bin. It must belong to the local authorities, for it was of the same shape and dimensions as those along the promenade.

Working on the principle that it was often possible to learn more about a man in five minutes by going through his rubbish than an hour spent with him in the charge-room, he lifted the orange lid and shone his torch inside. The black polythene liner bag looked dry. Underneath a layer of old *journaux* there was an assortment of odds and ends, mostly female; old tights, make-up, several padded coat-hangers, a large bag of greyish powder – it could have been some kind of talcum. It looked as though someone had been having a good clear-out. He poked around for a moment or two longer, but it was a waste of time. There was far too much clutter.

Another, much longer burst of applause came from the direction of the circus tent. The band broke out into a loud march. It sounded as though the show was nearing its end.

Acting on the spur of the moment, he lifted the plastic bag out of the container and carried it out to the car. Accustomed though he was to his master's vagaries, Pommes Frites did not look best pleased when it landed on the seat beside him.

'*Surveillez-le!*' Monsieur Pamplemousse gave him a quick pat, then hurried along the promenade in search of a suitable replacement bag.

It took him longer than he'd intended. The first two stank to high heaven, the third was nearly empty. He struck lucky at the fourth. A couple taking an evening stroll gave him an odd look when they saw what he was up to. He raised his hat and bade them a formal goodnight.

As he passed the car on his way back Monsieur Pamplemousse decided to risk Pommes Frites' displeasure once again by getting rid of the bag of ballast which was still on the back

89

seat. Slipping the new polythene liner into the container outside the caravan, he stuffed the much-chewed bag in the bottom and covered it with some paper, plumping it up to give it more bulk. Then he closed the lid. It wasn't quite as good as he would have liked, but it was the best he could manage in the time.

By the time Monsieur Pamplemousse had finished the first of the audience were already hurrying out, anxious to reach their cars before the main rush. Lights began to come on all around him; engines roared.

He hovered for a moment or two, wondering whether to go back to his car or stay for a little while longer. He decided to stay. The fair was coming alive again. The trickle of people leaving the circus had turned into a flood, all pushing and jostling to be first. It would be some time before they dispersed.

He began to wish he'd brought Pommes Frites; at least it would have ensured a free passage through the mass of people. As it was, the very fact that he was going against the main stream was resented. Skirting round the outside of the crowd, he made his way past a row of caravans in the direction of the menhir. Almost immediately he regretted the decision. He'd been so intent on avoiding other people he failed to see a figure lurking under the trees. It was the old harridan he'd encountered earlier in the day. To his horror, as soon as she saw him coming she started to wave and began hurrying towards him.

Almost without thinking he made a dive between two of the caravans, turned sharp left at the far end and doubled back up the other side. Peering round the corner, he was just in time to see the wretched woman disappear down the route he had just taken. Clearly she wasn't giving up in a hurry. Given the incredible complications of her attire, she had a surprising turn of speed. If she kept going at her present rate, there wasn't a moment to lose.

If he took a chance and followed on behind he ran the risk of finding her lying in wait. If he tried mingling with the crowd and she caught up with him it could be even worse. He would get no sympathy; from the look of some of them they were much more likely to egg her on.

Seeing a light coming from Madame Caoutchouc's caravan he made a dive for the steps. Mounting them in one bound, he flung open the door, then closed it gently behind him. Remaining where he was for a moment or two, hardly daring to breathe, he put his ear to one of the panels. To his relief there was no pounding of feet, no sound of anyone approaching.

Relaxing a little, he let go of the door handle and took in his surroundings. The black curtains were now drawn back, turning what had in effect been a series of compartments into one large room. The little table just inside the door had gone and the crystal ball was now on top of the hi-fi. He could hear the sound of running water coming from behind the door he'd noticed that morning. Madame Caoutchouc must be having a well-earned shower. The crocheted counterpane on the bed was littered with the impedimenta of her act; unidentifiable garments covered with sequins, the cup and saucer and the coffee-maker she'd used in her act, a top hat, a white towelling dressing-gown. The flowered dressing gown was lying discarded on the floor. On top of it was a whip.

To his right between the door and the sink unit was a small window. He was about to look out through a gap in the curtains when he heard the water in the shower being turned off. Abruptly the door at the far end swung open.

Madame Caoutchouc patently wasn't expecting visitors. When she caught sight of Monsieur Pamplemousse she stopped dead in her tracks and gave a gasp. Then, as she recognised him, she reached for the towelling dressing gown.

'What do you want? Didn't you see the *Fermé* notice? I am closed for the night.' She came towards him and reached for the door handle.

Monsieur Pamplemousse raised his hat. He decided to come clean. There was no great point in concocting a story.

'*Pardonnez-moi, Madame.* It is an inexcusable intrusion.

The truth is, there is someone outside I would rather not see. If I may just check first . . .' He motioned towards the window. 'I will not stay a moment longer than is necessary.'

'In that case I had better turn off the light, otherwise you will be seen.' Madame Caoutchouc essayed a brief and not altogether successful attempt at pulling her dressing-gown around her. Monsieur Pamplemousse averted his gaze and found himself looking at her image in the crystal ball. Her reflection as she reached for the switch near the door was distorted beyond belief.

'*Merci*. You are very kind.' He groped his way towards the window and slowly parted the curtains in the middle. The old woman was still there, skulking in the shadow of a nearby tree. From the way she was standing it looked as though she was quite prepared for a long wait.

He felt a large breast against his right shoulder. 'I can only see an old *clocharde*. Surely . . .'

'That is the one.'

'*Oooh, là, là*! I understand why you would not wish to see her.' There was a slight pause for thought. 'Why did she pick on you?'

'I do not know. Perhaps it is my aftershave.' He meant it as a joke, but it immediately reminded him of the scent the old crone had left behind outside the restaurant. Until that moment it had slipped his memory.

He tried concentrating on the view outside, but it wasn't easy. For someone well into her prime, Madame Caout-chouc's breast was surprisingly, not to say disturbingly, firm. Perhaps wrestling with crocodiles was good for the mammary glands. She was also either supremely unaware of the fact – which he very much doubted – or she was being deliberately slow in removing it. It was not only surprisingly firm, it was also remarkably damp. In fact, he was conscious of creeping dampness all down his back, and he was about to let go of the curtain when he felt her stiffen. A moment later he realised why. Christoph had come into view. The old woman evidently saw him too, for she slunk back even deeper into the shadows as he went past.

Madame Caoutchouc also drew back as she followed his progress. '*Salaud!*' The word was spat out with surprising venom.

His interest roused, Monsieur Pamplemousse craned to see where Christoph was going. In an effort to get a better view he tried standing on a shadowy object on the floor below the window. It felt soft and yielding beneath his feet and he nearly lost his balance.

Something came up and hit the side of his leg. He tried to brush it away. It felt soft and clammy. Instinctively he drew back.

'*Merde!*'

'*Attendez!*' Madame Caoutchouc pulled him away from the window and bent down. '*Attention au crocodile!*'

'*Un crocodile!*' Monsieur Pamplemousse jumped in horror, hardly able to believe his ears.

Staggering back, he scrabbled at empty air, then toppled forward, colliding with Madame Caoutchouc as she stood up. As he clutched at her he felt himself enveloped in a damp but heady mixture compounded of flesh and fabric. It was so sudden and unexpected it was all he could do to stay upright. He was vaguely aware of making a futile grab for his hat as it slid off the back of his head – the more bizarre the situation the more man clung to the most trivial of possessions – then there was a crash of breaking glass as they collided with the table and the vase of flowers went flying. Spinning away from it, they hovered uncertainly in the middle of the caravan, then landed on the bed in a panting heap of twisted arms and legs.

He tried desperately to disentangle himself, but his body seemed to be held in place by a vice-like grip from which there was no escape. It was like a bad dream. Arms encircled him. Toes dug into his spine. Toes – or was it the coffee pot? Perhaps even – heaven forbid – perhaps even even the crocodile – it was hard to tell. He had temporarily lost all feeling.

Nothing Madame Caoutchouc had done in the circus ring could possibly have prepared him for the complexity of their present arrangements. Had he been forewarned he might have been better prepared. Like a swimmer about to attempt a swallow dive from the high board, he would have filled his lungs with sufficient life-giving air to enable him to surface unharmed. As it was, all the breath had been squeezed out of him during the first few moments of their embrace and his lungs were now so tightly compressed the prospect of refilling them seemed remote in the extreme.

He called out and heard a thin voice remarkably unlike his own somewhere in the distance. There was a tramp of feet and then other voices too; voices he didn't recognise, uttering imprecations and oaths. Cries of '*Quelle horreur!*' and 'She has had an attack of her old complaint!' impinged on his brain. Hands reached out, grasping at anything within reach, in a vain attempt to pull them apart.

At the height of it all there was a loud banging sound. It seemed to be coming from outside the caravan. Irrationally it occurred to him that it might even be the old woman. The one he had been trying to escape from. It would be an ironic twist of fate if she came to his rescue, but by that time he hardly cared.

The knocking ceased and there was a blinding flash of light. It was followed by a familiar voice calling out his name. He told himself it wasn't possible. It had to be part of some dreadful nightmare from which he would wake at any moment. But as he twisted his head round to look his heart sank. Patently his senses had not entirely deserted him. His worst fears had been realised.

'*Incroyable!*' In his delivery of that one word the Director managed to convey a variety of thoughts and emotions: shock, disbelief, reprehension, condemnation – a shorter word would hardly have sufficed. Pommes Frites, who was standing beside him, very wisely remained silent.

'*Monsieur le Directeur, bonsoir! Comment ça va?*' Fearful of getting a crick in his neck, Monsieur Pamplemousse lay back and having delivered himself of such pleasantries as he could manage in the circumstances, sought refuge behind the fleshy ramparts of Madame Caoutchouc.

Carefully avoiding a large breast suspended perilously close to his right eye, he took in the scene above and around him. It was one which would have caused Degas, that occasional chronicler of circus life, to reach hastily for his brush, lest he miss a golden opportunity which might never repeat itself. Although, given the confined space of the caravan, even he might have paused for a moment in order to wonder if it was too crowded a scene for his canvas.

The semi-naked figure of a woman astride a man lying on a bed; a midget dressed as a clown tugging at her left arm, a bearded lady tugging at her right; discarded sequin-covered garments strewn about the floor; and in the foreground, its mouth open wide as though it, too, could hardly believe its eyes . . . a rubber crocodile.

'You may well hide your face in shame, Pamplemousse,' boomed the Director. 'I knew from the tenor of our conversation on the telephone yesterday that something was amiss, but little did I dream as I was journeying down here today, nor when I came across your car parked on the esplanade, that I would find you in this . . . this . . .' For once the Director was at a loss for words.

Looking around the caravan his gaze alighted on the crystal ball. 'It does not need the services of a soothsayer, Pamplemousse, to deduce that your future looks black, very black indeed. Perhaps, when you can tear yourself away, and when you have a spare moment, you would care to take a look in that ball yourself and tell me what you see. You are one of my most trusted employees, here on a mission of utmost importance, a mission, the outcome of which I need hardly say, affects us all. And what do I find? You are so engrossed in satisfying the desires of the flesh you cannot even bother to observe the basic courtesies of life by standing when I enter the room. I shall await your pleasure at the Ty Coz.'

Monsieur Pamplemousse took a deep breath and poked his head out again. 'One moment, *Monsieur*. I can explain it all . . .'

95

But the Director had already stalked out. One by one the others crept silently after him until only Pommes Frites and Madame Caoutchouc were left; the one out of loyalty, the other for reasons best known to herself.

Pommes Frites looked somewhat aggrieved; not so much with those around him as with the injustice of the world in general. In tracking his master down, in sniffing out his trail amongst all the others and following it to the bitter end, he'd only been doing what he thought was a good deed. Praise would normally have been his due. As it was he sensed that for the second time that day he had put his foot in it, and on this occasion not just one, but all four. His master didn't look best pleased. It really wasn't fair, but as he knew all too well from past experience, the Goddess in charge of fairness did not bestow her bounties in any logical order, but scattered them far and wide in random fashion. For a brief moment he was tempted to give the piece of anatomy nearest to him a conciliatory lick, but he thought better of it. Without the benefit of a closer inspection, it was hard to tell which bits belonged to his master and which belonged to his companion of the moment.

Having decided that praise was not to be his lot, and keeping a wary eye on the crocodile, Pommes Frites settled himself down to await developments. No doubt things would sort themselves out in due course. They usually did.

'*C'est un trouduc!*'

'Now, *Madame*,' Monsieur Pamplemousse hoped the Director hadn't lingered outside. He doubted whether he would like hearing himself being called a silly old fart. He made another attempt to break free. 'Perhaps you could release me?'

'I am sorry, *Monsieur*. That is not possible.'

'Not possible! What do you mean, not possible?'

'It is as Emilio said, I have an attack of my old complaint. It happens occasionally. The last time was in Lille. It is a kind of a seizure, a form of cramp.'

'Cramp?' repeated Monsieur Pamplemousse. 'An indiarubber woman with cramp?'

'It is what the doctors call *un risque du métier*: an occu-pational hazard. I am not as young as I used to be. I think perhaps it is the sea air. The damp has entered my bones.'

'How long do they last, these attacks?'

'Poof!' Monsieur Pamplemousse wished he hadn't asked. Clearly, Madame Caoutchouc's thought processes involved physical as well as mental effort. He waited for the heaving to stop.

'Sometimes only a few minutes. Sometimes for several hours. In Lille it lasted all one night!'

All one night! In Lille! It was tempting to suggest that if she was so good at looking into the future the least she could do would be to sort out when he would be free, but that would have been unkind. The pain under his right shoulder was getting worse. Wriggling his left arm free he managed to twist round and feel between himself and the bedding. He with-drew a large cylindrical metal object.

'If you have a match,' said Madame Caoutchouc, 'I could make you some *café*. It would mean boiling a kettle. The *café* I make in the ring is only a trick. We could roll to the *cuisine* together.'

'I think not, *merci*.' He could envisage many more profit-able ways of spending the next ten minutes than by waiting for a kettle to boil – especially with Pommes Frites looking on, watching their every move. He suddenly didn't feel thirsty any more.

'You could tell me what first gave you the idea for a crocodile made of rubber,' he suggested.

'Have you tried keeping a real crocodile, *Monsieur*?'

He shook his head.

'It is not easy in a caravan.'

As a statement of fact it was unanswerable.

'The lighting was my late husband's idea.'

'It works very well. I would never have known.'

As conversation lapsed once again, Monsieur Pample-mousse allowed his mind to drift. He wondered if he should suggest turning on the radio, but that would also involve moving. He couldn't even ask if she had read any good books lately.

'Cramp is a question of tensions.' Madame Caoutchouc was the first to speak. 'Sometimes, when things are going badly, I feel them coming on.'

'I understand.'

Monsieur Pamplemousse relaxed. Despite everything, he felt a great tenderness come over him. 'The greatest pains,' he said gently, 'are those you cannot tell others about. Perhaps what you need most of all at this moment is to relieve your tensions.'

Madame Caoutchouc looked around. 'If only I could reach my whip,' she said. 'I might be able to turn out the light.'

Monsieur Pamplemousse caught Pommes Frites' eye. He pointed towards the floor. 'I know a magic word:

'Fetch!'

Pommes Frites rose to his feet. Ever alive to the needs of others, anxious to make amends for past mistakes, he had the self-satisfied air of a dog who knew that if he waited long enough his hour would come. It was not for him to reason why his master should want to share his bed with a rubber crocodile.

Monsieur Pamplemousse heaved a deep sigh as something cold and slimy landed by his side. All the signs pointed to the fact that it was going to be a very long night.

6

THE MORNING AFTER

It was some time after dawn when Monsieur Pamplemousse finally woke. The sun was streaming in through a gap in the curtains. He looked at his watch. It showed just after seven o'clock. Moving gently so as not to disturb the figure beside him, he started to get dressed. By rights he should have felt terrible, but in fact he had slept soundly for several hours; the best sleep he'd had for a long time. Before then they had both talked far into the night. Talk had induced relaxation, and relaxation had brought with it release followed by oblivion.

Pommes Frites stirred, opened one eye to observe his master at work, then stood up and noisily shook himself. The sound woke Madame Caoutchouc.

'You are going?'

Monsieur Pamplemousse looked at her reflection in the mirror as he finished straightening his tie. 'I must.'

'You won't stay for a *café*?'

He shook his head. 'I have a lot of work to get through.' There would be a good deal of explaining to do as well and he was anxious to get back to the hotel before the Director was up and about. All that apart, without wishing to offend Madame Caoutchouc, he didn't want to be seen leaving the fairground, let alone her caravan. For no particular reason he had a sudden mental picture of Doucette waiting for him outside. It reminded him that he had not yet posted her a card.

Madame Caoutchouc reached up and took hold of his hand as he crossed to the bed. 'Then I shall not see you again?'

'Who knows? It is a small world.' He was tempted to embroider his reply with promises he knew he had no intention of keeping; to visit the circus in another town perhaps, but he thought better of it.

She pulled his hand towards her and held it for a brief moment against her breast, then lifted it higher still, looking first at his thumb, then at each of the fingers in turn.

'Your thumb shows strength and determination. It also shows you can be stubborn.'

Monsieur Pamplemousse remembered now. Like the Chinese and Indians, Gypsies placed great store on the thumb, as indeed did many Christians. To them it was a symbol of God.

'Yet the joints of your fingers are well formed, which means you are thoughtful and seek harmony. You also have a strong sense of justice. It is an interesting hand.'

She ran a finger slowly across the palm of his hand. 'You have a long life line – but take care.'

'I always take care. Life becomes more finite and therefore more precious the older one gets.'

'If you were staying longer I could tell your fortune.'

'I think I would rather not know. To be aware of one's character by the star sign is one thing. That I believe in. But to try and look into the future is something else again. It is like a mother knowing the sex of her unborn child.'

He raised her hand to his lips. Her fingers felt warm and pliant. He gave them a squeeze. '*Au revoir.*'

'*Au revoir*, and *merci.*'

Halfway across the site he turned to look back and saw her wave. The curtains were still drawn in Christoph's caravan. A few workers clearing up the site gave him curious glances as he left.

The tide was out and the beach was almost deserted. Someone was exercising a dog at the far end. A small boy was out with his father trying unsuccessfully to fly a kite. Halfway along, a man was raking the sand smooth outside a beach café. A few fishermen were digging for worms. Two nuns taking an early morning stroll watched as he made his way down some steps. For some reason best known to themselves they made the sign of the cross. One of them whispered something behind her hand and the other laughed.

Pommes Frites galloped across the gleaming wet sand, sniffed the sea, then came running back, full of the joys of summer. Monsieur Pamplemousse picked up a piece of driftwood and threw it for him.

He now felt he knew all there was to know about circuses; in particular the Circus Bretagno; how it started, its family history, where they had been to, where they were going – and where they had planned to go before the accident; the cost of keeping a show on the road; the dramas and scandals.

Of Christoph he knew very little more, other than that he came from one of the Greek islands and had arrived on the scene just over a year ago looking for work. They had been in Italy at the time. Madame Caoutchouc had been widowed only a few months earlier and was finding the task of running a circus by herself more than she could cope with. People needed to be paid, bookings made, advertisements placed. To be sure she had the children, Yasmin and her younger sister, but they already had more than enough on their plate. The prospect of another man to help out – an intelligent one at that – seemed heaven-sent.

At first everything in the circus had ben lovely. He was tall, dark, handsome, with a mop of black, curly hair, and the inevitable happened; in a very short space of time Yasmin had fallen head over heels in love. Christoph proposed to her, and soon afterwards they were married between shows in Trieste. The BMW had been a wedding gift; the caravan arrived soon after. He'd turned up with it out of the blue shortly after the honeymoon. Any misgivings Madame Caoutchouc might have felt she kept to herself, especially when he gave her the hi-fi. It had become her pride and joy.

Pommes Frites returned with the wood. Monsieur Pamplemousse threw it for him again, further this time. It landed with a splash in a hollow left by the outgoing tide.

It wasn't until some time after the wedding that things started to go wrong. Christoph had begun to show signs of moodiness, often disappearing for days at a time. In any other job that would have been bad enough, but in the circus it was unforgivable. When he was there he threw his weight around, which gave rise to ill-feeling. He also began interfering in other ways, criticising their itinerary and going into sulks if it wasn't altered to suit him. Their present booking was typical. By rights the circus should still be in the Ardennes, not reaching Brittany until August when the holiday season would be at its peak. But once again he had got his way.

What was the phrase she had used? It was the reverse of 'you could drop him in a pig-sty and he would still come up smelling of roses'; rather, 'you could cover him with honey and he would still smell of tar'. There was obviously no love lost between them. Rightly or wrongly she was blaming him for Yasmin's accident.

Calling Pommes Frites to heel, Monsieur Pamplemousse made his way back to the car. The plastic bag was still on the back seat. It was probably too obvious what it was for anyone to bother stealing it. Thankfully, he had left the camera tucked underneath it out of sight.

As they drove past the Quai Général de Gaulle he caught sight of a small group of fishermen already hard at work repairing their blue sardine nets. Others were attending to their lobster pots. They were probably all well fortified with an early-morning *marc* or two. He wouldn't have minded joining them.

At the Ty Coz he parked in the same space between the two large English cars, but once again his hopes of slipping into the hotel unobserved were doomed. The main door was still locked. The owner himself appeared in response to the bell. He eyed the plastic bag over Monsieur Pamplemousse's shoulder with some disfavour.

'*Petit déjeuner* is not until *huit heures*.'

'That,' said Monsieur Pamplemousse with some asperity, 'is why we have brought our own. We are both very hungry.' It was a cheap joke, but it made him feel better as he turned and crossed the hall. He should have asked for two plates. Half expecting to find the Director lying in wait for him, he hurried up the stairs to his room.

Bathed and shaved, he spread some paper over the bed and emptied the plastic bag over the top. Spread out, the contents looked even more of a jumble. There was something slightly depressing about handling someone else's personal belongings; it felt like an intrusion. Shoes were somehow especially evocative. One by one he put everything back into the bag until he was left with a few items of interest: several lengths of wire, multi-stranded in a variety of colours – of the kind that came in flat ribbons and was used in electronic equipment, a plain white packet containing the remains of some whitish flakes, a small plain paper bag which had once contained some white powder (he tried some between his fingers and it felt like chalk), an unused length of multi-core solder, several more pieces of sawn-off fibreglass – similar to the piece he had found on his first visit to the circus, the larger bag of greyish powder he'd come across the previous evening, two paint brushes (although the bristles had gone hard on the outside they had both been used recently and looked as though they had been bought for the job – the metal round the base of the handle was still shiny), and a small unlabelled screw-capped bottle containing traces of a colourless liquid.

Before Monsieur Pamplemousse had a chance to sniff the contents of the bottle there was a knock on the door. Hastily gathering up the remains of the things on the bed, he put them into a drawer in his beside cabinet. He was only just in time. There was an impatient rattle of the handle, then the door opened.

It was the Director. He was dressed in his yachting outfit: matching dark blue hat and blazer, the latter sporting buttons bearing the Christian Dior motif, white shirt with a knotted scarf in lighter blue, and matching two-tone blue and white rubber-soled shoes. A vision of sartorial elegance, his expression as he gazed around the room was a mixture of surprise and distaste.

'Pamplemousse, don't tell me your salary is so inadequate you have to resort to sifting through the contents of a garbage bag before you are able to face the world?'

Monsieur Pamplemousse resisted the temptation to say 'yes'. He had no wish to upset the apple-cart quite so early in the day.

'I was looking for a bone for Pommes Frites, *Monsieur*,' he said simply. 'Like me, he hasn't entirely taken to *La Cuisine Règionale Naturelle*.' He tried to avoid Pommes Frites' gaze as he uttered the words. It wasn't easy. Pommes Frites had an uncanny knack of knowing when he was avoiding the truth.

'Ah, yes.' The Director barely registered the reply. He seemed slightly ill at ease.

Monsieur Pamplemousse waited for the blasting which he felt could be heading his way. But either sleep had worked wonders, or second thoughts had prevailed. He strongly suspected the latter. With only a day to go before the launch the Director wouldn't want to run the risk of his walking out on the whole operation. His next remark was mild in the extreme.

'I suggest, Aristide, that if you feel up to it we drive into town and take our *petit déjeuner* at one of those little cafés near the port.'

'*Monsieur* would not prefer to stay in the hotel? I understood it was highly recommended.'

'No, Pamplemousse, I think not. It is a lovely morning and I'm sure the fresh air will do us both the world of good.'

Monsieur Pamplemousse followed the Director out of the hotel, deposited the plastic bag in the back of his 2CV, then held open the rear door of the Director's car so that Pommes Frites could climb in.

Pommes Frites gazed round approvingly while his master got into the front seat, then he settled himself down in order to make the most of things while they lasted. Soft music issued from a loudspeaker by his ear; music as soft in its way as the leather beneath him.

'*Au revoir, à bientôt.*' The Director replaced a telephone receiver and switched on the ignition. The engine purred into life. He glanced across at Monsieur Pamplemousse. 'Work, Aristide. Work must go on. I have just telephoned headquarters to tell them to stand by for further instructions. Time is disappearing rapidly. It is Thursday already.'

Monsieur Pamplemousse made a suitable noise in reply. The picture of everyone standing by their office desks was not an easy one to focus on. Even more difficult, for experience told him where the conversation was leading, was finding a suitable answer to what he knew would be the next question. He wondered whether it would come on the journey into Port St. Augustin, or during *petit déjeuner* itself. Guessing it was likely to be the latter he closed his eyes and concentrated his mind, hoping he wouldn't be disturbed before inspiration came his way. His hopes did not go unrewarded. Hardly had they left Ty Coz than the telephone rang and the Director was once again immersed in his problems. This time it had to do with some printing technicality. It was a welcome diversion.

At a little café by the harbour they ordered *jus d'orange* and *café* for two. After some deliberation, Monsieur Pamplemousse chose a *pain au sucre* and a *brioche* for himself and a *pain au chocolat* for Pommes Frites. The Director called for a plate of *croissants*. Then, remembering his diet, reluctantly changed the order to one.

After the rain, everything looked clean and newly washed. The cars had not yet started to arrive. The only sound came from a few seagulls wheeling and diving overhead as they greeted the arrival of a fishing boat. Further along the *quai* the men were still repairing their nets.

Blissfully unaware that his symbol in *Le Guide* was at stake – a bar stool indicating above-average food and service – the *patron* won bonus points for bringing fresh orange juice without being asked. He gained several more when he returned a moment later carrying a bowl of water for Pommes Frites. There were two ice cubes floating on the surface. It was good to have their judgement confirmed.

The Director waited until the crunching had died down, then he cleared his throat.

'Ah, Pamplemousse, this is the life.'

'*Oui, Monsieur.*' Monsieur Pamplemousse broke a *brioche* in two and automatically handed the other half down below the table top. He felt a comforting wet nose, then both disappeared.

'It is a pity, Pamplemousse, that life cannot always be *croissants* and *café*.'

'*Oui, Monsieur.*'

'And circuses.'

'*Oui, Monsieur.*'

A look of slight irritation flitted across the Director's face as he realised that he was to get no help whatsoever. Draining his cup, he dabbed at his lips with a paper serviette and embarked on a different course.

'Tell me, Aristide, in between bouts of . . .' Monsieur Pamplemousse sat and listened respectfully while the Director broke into a series of whistles and grunts which were clearly meant to embrace a multitude of sins, most of which were impossible to put into words. 'Did you . . . er, did you manage to give any thought to the matter in hand?'

Monsieur Pamplemousse breathed a sigh of relief. The assault he had feared was not about to materialise. 'I thought of very little else, *Monsieur.*'

The Director looked at him uneasily, clearly wondering whether or not he had been misunderstood. 'I suppose,' he continued after a suitable pause, 'that in time one gets a little blasé. What, may I ask, were your conclusions?'

Monsieur Pamplemousse placed the tips of his fingers together, forming a steeple with his hands which reflected that of the nearby parish church. He closed his eyes. The sun felt warm to his face, reminding him that he should take care.

He was not by nature a sun-worshipper.

'If I may say so, *Monsieur*, your menu was a work of art.'

'You think so, Aristide?' The Director sounded better pleased.

'*Oui, Monsieur*. It was like a noble wine. It had . . .' Monsieur Pamplemousse paused for a moment while he sought the right words. 'It had completeness and roundness and fullness. It had flavour; rich without being cloying, it had finesse.' He wondered for a moment if he was overdoing things, but the Director's next words dispelled any such doubts.

'Then you think we should go ahead, Aristide?'

'*Non, Monsieur*.' He braced himself. It was the *moment critique*. 'With the greatest respect, I think the answer has to be *non*. It would, in its way, be too perfect.' Another way of putting it would be that with such a weight of food on board, the dirigible would never leave the ground, but he resisted the temptation. It was a moment for tact.

'Such a meal should be reserved for another, perhaps even greater, occasion: a State Banquet *par exemple*. It should not, indeed *must not*, be wasted. The great problem as I see it is that with so many other things to occupy their minds, the guests may not give it their undivided attention. They would be placed in a constant state of dilemma. It would be sacrilege to allow the *langouste* or the *canard* to grow cold, but supposing, just supposing at the very moment of their being served, the dirigible happened to be passing over somewhere like Josselin, with its magnificent castle, or crossing the Côte d'Emeraude . . . It would be a tragedy if in enjoying *Les Six Gloires de la France Culinaire* they had to forgo some of the glories which lie beneath.'

He could tell by the silence that his point had gone home.

'You are quite right, Pamplemousse. I must confess that in the excitement of composition that point had escaped me.'

There was another, even longer silence.

'Do you have any suggestions, Aristide?'

'I have been giving the matter a great deal of consideration,

Monsieur.' It was true. All the way down from the hotel he had thought of little else.

'Given all that I have just said, and bearing in mind that space is strictly limited, I feel our keynote should be simplicity. That simplicity, *Monsieur*, which is synonymous with the quiet good taste and that dedication to perfection for perfection's sake, which has always been a hallmark of *Le Guide*.

'I suggest we start with some smoked salmon from Scotland.'

'*Saumon fumé?*'

'*Oui, Monsieur.*'

'From *Ecosse* rather than from France?'

'*Oui, Monsieur.*'

The Director gave a snort. 'Then one thing is certain, Pamplemousse. The view from the dirigible will not be wasted. I must say I am a little disappointed.'

'*Monsieur*, again with respect, the eyes of the world will be upon us, and it will be seen as a gesture of good will, an example of that lack of chauvinism for which we French are renowned. That apart, in my humble opinion there is little to equal *saumon* which has been *fumé* over a peat fire in Scotland. It is their one great contribution to the world of *cuisine* and more than makes up for haggis.

'It will, of course, need to be wild *saumon*, pink from feeding on shellfish and not from some chemical colouring agent in their food pellets. I am told much of the *saumon* we eat these days is farmed and that there are people who have never actually tasted the real thing. And with it, some lemon juice and a little fresh bread with butter from Normandy. The whole washed down with a suitable chilled champagne, perhaps a bottle or two of Gosset.'

'And then?'

Detecting overtones of gathering interest in the Director's voice, Monsieur Pamplemousse pressed home his advantage.

'You mentioned Fauchon at one point in your letter, *Monsieur*. It was in connection with the dessert. May I ask how many times you have tried to walk past their windows in the Place de la Madeleine and failed in the attempt, your attention caught by some exquisite arrangement of delicacies: a *tableau* of crabs and *pâtés* in one window, *terrines* and hams in another; *soufflés* juxtaposed with *fraises des bois* in a third? In short, all the ingredients for a picnic the like of which could not be assembled anywhere else in the world, and all of them but a telephone call away.'

'A picnic, Aristide?' Opening one eye, Monsieur Pamplemousse was just in time to catch the Director licking his lips. He had suspected as much. 'That is an excellent idea. Simple, and yet so right; in keeping with the spirit of the enterprise itself. And you would finish the meal how?'

'*Monsieur*, a good meal is like a well-written story. Interest has to be captured as early as possible, the main part should be satisfying, and the ending should be on a high note leaving the reader both happy and yet wishing for more. Replete, yet still hungry.'

'One moment, Aristide. Before we go any further –' The Director clicked his fingers for the waiter. 'Another *pain au sucre*? Or a *brioche*? I think I may indulge in a further *croissant* myself. All this talk of food is making me feel hungry. No doubt Pommes Frites could toy with a second *pain au chocolat*?'

'He has never let me down yet, *Monsieur*.'

'*Encore!*' With a single grand gesture, the Director managed to embrace the whole of their erstwhile breakfast.

The fishing-boat was starting to unload its catch; baskets full of sea-bass and sole landed on the *quai*, others were filled with a mixture of oddities. A few gnarled faces gathered in a small group to watch. A nun on a *Vélocette* drew up outside the P.T.T. and went inside. A car with a sailing boat in tow went past and disappeared onto the beach. Far out to sea a small flotilla of boats from the sailing school lay becalmed, waiting with resignation for the wind to freshen. Nothing in life was perfect.

'Now, Pamplemousse,' the Director could hardly conceal

his impatience as the waiter disappeared again. 'Tell me about your *pièce de résistance*, your *coup de maître*.'

'It is a dish, *Monsieur*, which Madame Pamplemousse reserves for special occasions. It is called *Sabayon aux Pêches*. It is both simple and elegant and although it only requires the simplest of apparatus, there is a certain theatricality about its preparation which always heightens the effect.

'First, fresh ripe peaches are cooked in water to which sugar and the juice of half a lemon has been added. When they are tender, the skin is removed and each peach is placed in a large Cognac balloon.

'The *Sabayon* is made with a mixture of egg yolks and sugar, to which some liqueur have been added – Madame Pamplemousse always uses Marsala, but others prefer Grand Marnier or apricot brandy or even champagne. It should be whisked by hand in a *bain-marie* over a low heat until the mixture begins to ribbon, then left to simmer. At the appropriate moment it is reheated and whisked again until it fluffs up into the consistency of softly whipped cream. Then it is spooned over the peaches and served. The result, Monsieur, is pure ambrosia. It never fails to bring forth gasps of admiration, especially when accompanied by a glass of Sauternes. I would suggest a Château d'Yquem. It would, perhaps, be too much to hope for a 1904 – the year in which *entente cordiale* was born – but that was a great vintage and it would be a beautiful ending to the meal.'

'Aristide,' under the pretence of removing a speck of dust from his right eye, the Director wiped away the suspicion of a tear, 'words fail me. I have to admit that when I first arrived down here I began to entertain severe doubts concerning the wisdom of entrusting you with this mission. I had almost decided to take charge of the operation myself. But all is forgiven. It is easy enough to strike a note when asked, but to hit exactly the right one at precisely the right moment is another matter entirely. It requires that touch of God-given genius which few of us are lucky enough to possess. Leave the wine to me. In the meantime I will send for Madame

Pamplemousse at once.'

Monsieur Pamplemousse gave a start. 'I hardly think that will be necessary, *Monsieur*.' The thought of Doucette arriving in Port St. Augustin filled him with alarm, especially while the circus was still in town. She might even want to be taken there. Innocent though his encounter with Madame Caoutchouc had been – a case of cause and effect – explanations would not be easy should it come to light.

'Come, come, Aristide. You said yourself that the dish is one of her specialities. Simple though you make it sound, we cannot afford to have things go wrong. Eggs can curdle; pans can catch fire. To end on a low note would be little short of disaster. We must take no risks.'

'I think, *Monsieur*, that if you send for Madame Pamplemousse you will be taking a very grave risk indeed. Curdled eggs could be the least of your problems. Madame Pamplemousse has never flown before and if she found herself in a dirigible cooking for Heads of State she might well go to pieces.'

'Then whom do we ask, Pamplemousse? As I have already told you, Bocuse is in Japan, Vergé is in America. Time is not on our side.'

For the second time that morning Monsieur Pamplemousse closed his eyes as he sought inspiration, and once again luck did not desert him.

'On my way down, *Monsieur*,' he said, after a moment's pause, 'Pommes Frites and I made a small detour . . .'

The Director listened intently while Monsieur Pamplemousse described his meal, only occasionally interjecting over some technical detail or asking for elaboration of a particular dish.

'I think,' said Monsieur Pamplemousse, when he had finished describing his jam omelette for the fourth time, 'to have such a person in charge of the *cuisine* will not only be a *plume* in our *chapeau* – for he is a name as yet undiscovered by our rivals – it will also be living proof of that great strength which is France; the miracle that right across our land, in the cities and in the smallest villages, such talent exists as naturally and as unremarked as the fact that day follows night.'

'Pamplemousse, I have said it all before. To repeat it would be an embarrassment, but if you are doing nothing for *déjeuner* today we could meet and you could tell me about it all over again.

'There is also the matter of the circus. You may not wish to talk about it of course, and if so, I fully understand. I will respect your wishes to the full. But I must confess it kept me awake a good deal during the night. Images kept forming in my mind.

'I have always considered myself a man of the world. Not, of course, as experienced as your good self in the more esoteric pursuits, but we all have different tastes. It would be a very dull place if we didn't.

'Tell me, Aristide, was she . . . er . . . was she very . . . *pneumatique*? Presumably she is not called *Madame Caout-chouc* for nothing.'

'She is a little like a child's india-rubber, *Monsieur*. She has both a hard and a soft side.'

The Director nodded. 'And the crocodile?'

'That too, was surprisingly pliable.'

'How strange. It is a variation I had not heard of before. Visits to the zoo with my young nephew will never seem quite the same again.'

'I doubt, *Monsieur*, if I shall ever look a crocodile straight in the eye again either.'

Monsieur Pamplemousse replied absentmindedly. With-drawing the Leitz Trinovid binoculars from his jacket pocket, he trained them on a distant figure at the far end of the promenade. As the image came into sharp focus he jumped to his feet.

'*Merde!*'

'*Pardon*, Pamplemousse?' The Director looked startled.

'I am afraid, *Monsieur, déjeuner* will not be possible after all. There is work to be done. I must telephone Fauchon; also the chef I was telling you about. There is the printing of the menu to be arranged. Facilities for the *cuisine* must be organised.'

'The telephone in my car is at your disposal, Aristide.' The Director felt in his pocket for the keys.

'With respect, *Monsieur*,' Monsieur Pamplemousse glanced anxiously along the promenade – the old hag was getting nearer, 'they will all take time. I think it will be cheaper in the long run if I make them from a call box. I will get myself a new *carte*.'

'Ah, Aristide,' the Director tempered his obvious disappointment with a beam of approval. 'If only Madame Grante were with us now to hear you say that. I am sure she would . . .' He broke off and gazed in horror at the approaching figure. 'Pamplemousse, that person is waving at us! Don't tell me, I can scarcely credit it. Is there no end to your intrigues?'

'I think it must be you she is after, *Monsieur*. Perhaps she is in need of a lift.'

Oblivious to the Director's protestations Monsieur Pamplemousse signalled to Pommes Frites and together they hastened along the *quai* in the direction of the shopping precinct. It wasn't until they reached the safety of the shadows from the overhanging gables that he paused to see if they were being followed. Slipping into a shop doorway, he turned and looked back the way they had come, but the old woman was nowhere in sight. Perhaps even now she was importuning the Director.

There were occasions when retreat was definitely the better part of valour, and the present situation was one of them. Besides, the walk back to the hotel would do them both good and there was a lot to think about, not the least of which was the contents of the drawer in his room. Another trip to Nantes was indicated. After that? Who knew? It would all depend on the report of the chemist. Unless he was very much mistaken he had come across the classic recipe for manufacturing knock-out pills.

7

THE BALLOON GOES UP

The National Anthem of both countries had been played by a contingent from the French naval base at St. Nazaire, the parade had been reviewed, formal greetings had been exchanged in front of the dirigible for the benefit of the world's television cameras. A small group of children from a local school, dressed in traditional costume, performed a brief dance. Afterwards, a red, white and blue bouquet made up of poppies, cornflowers and marguerites was presented by the smallest child to the visiting Head of State. A battery of press photographers had recorded the event for posterity. Speeches of congratulation had been made, hopes for the future expressed, comparisons drawn between the present flight and that of an early pioneer, Monsieur Le Brix, an aviator from the Morbihan who in 1927, along with a Monsieur Costes, was the first to fly around the world.

Now, as lesser mortals withdrew to watch from a safe distance, the party got ready to board the airship. The ground crew, their white overalls immaculately pressed for the occasion, took the strain on the mooring ropes, although with only the lightest of breezes blowing it was scarcely necessary. The windsock hung limply from its pole, as did the flags of France and *Grande-Bretagne*.

Monsieur Pamplemousse could see Commander Winters

114

and Capitaine Leflaix watching anxiously from their cabin window as more photographs were taken, this time of the two leaders posing in turn at the top of the aluminium steps. Capitaine Leflaix would not be pleased; they were facing outwards. No doubt both he and Commander Winters would be glad when they were airborne. At least their illustrious passengers were in for a better flight than he'd had to endure. Apart from a few wisps of strato-cumulus to the south the sky was totally blue. He almost envied them the experience.

Not for the first time that morning, Monsieur Pamplemousse found his attention wandering. He had woken with a curious feeling in the pit of his stomach that all was not well. Pommes Frites, ever sensitive to his master's moods, had obviously caught it too. From the moment they arrived at the airstrip he had been twitchy. When he caught sight of the balloon he became even more ill at ease, no doubt fearing another parting of the ways. Monsieur Pamplemousse bent down and gave him a reassuring pat.

He cast his eyes round the field as he did so. Security was as tight now as it had been lax a few days before. There were police and guards everywhere, their guns at the ready, walkie-talkies working overtime. A dozen familiar dark blue vans of the *Sûreté Nationale* were parked discreetly under the trees. As always, those behind the barred windows, having been kept in a state of enforced idleness for many hours, would be more than ready to wade in and take it out on those nearest to hand should anything untoward happen to mar the occasion.

The crowd of sightseers had been carefully selected; representatives of local government in their best clothes; heads of fish and vegetable canneries mingled with their workers. Nurses in uniform stood alongside patients in wheelchairs; boilermakers from St. Nazaire hobnobbed with building workers. A group of ubiquitous nuns kept themselves slightly apart from the rest, as was their wont.

Monsieur Pamplemousse had a lot on his mind. Like Commander Winters and his crew, he couldn't wait for the take-off so that he could get down to other matters. His suspicions about the contents of the envelope had been confirmed by a chemist in Nantes. The bottle contained the remains of some ethyl-chlorate; the white powder was calcium carbonate – common chalk; the flakes were tragacanth – commonly used as a binding agent. In short, all the necessary ingredients for manufacturing knock-out pills. The question was, had Christoph given one to Yasmin? And if he had, why?

If she'd been given one before the performance it would almost certainly have brought on sleepiness. Had he perhaps miscalculated the dose? Perhaps he had been hoping it would take effect sooner than it did; that was the charitable explanation. But even so, the very fact of going to the trouble of making the pills in the first place suggested something more than a spur of the moment act.

There was still a query hanging over the light-grey powder in the plastic bag.

Monsieur Pamplemousse was roused from his thoughts as the airship's engines roared into life and the ground crew began removing the ballast bags. For a moment he had an uneasy feeling that Pommes Frites might take it into his head to indulge in another game of tug-of-war, but to his relief he seemed to have suddenly lost interest in the whole affair. He counted the bags; according to the handout there should be seven 10kg bags for each passenger. Fifty-six were removed. Complicated hand signals began between the cockpit and the ground-crew – they could have been selling stocks and shares in the Bourse for all the sense they made. A moment later, as the nose of the airship was released from its mooring, those manning the bow lines pulled the airship sideways towards a clear position ready for take-off.

Monsieur Pamplemousse's own camera had been working overtime. There would be no shortage of pictures to accompany his article in *Le Guide*'s staff magazine; rather the reverse. Having filled the frame with a close-up of well-known faces peering out of the cabin windows, he quickly changed to a wide-angle lens.

He was just in time. As the fans were rotated groundwards and the lines released, more power was applied to the engines. The naval contingent stood to attention, the band launched into 'Anchors Away', and a cheer went up from the assembled crowd as the dirigible rose into the air, nose down at first to ensure the lower tail fin didn't make contact with the ground, then levelling out as it gained height. Slowly it executed a long and gentle turn before heading out across the sea towards the Golfe du Morbihan.

As the spectators began to disperse, drifting back to their cars and *autobuses*, Monsieur Pamplemousse saw the Director heading his way. He must have travelled with a good deal of luggage, for he was even more immaculately dressed than usual; the rosette of the *Légion d'Honneur* awarded for his services to *haute cuisine* was displayed in the lapel of his exquisitely tailored dark blue suit.

'Congratulations, Aristide,' the Director held out his hand. 'I managed to feast my eyes on your handiwork and I must say it was impossible to fault. Taste buds will undoubtedly be titillated.'

'*Merci, Monsieur.* I see you were also successful with the Château d'Yquem.'

The Director looked pleased. 'I have my sources.' Clearly they were not about to be revealed.

'You tested the food personally, of course? It would be most unfortunate if it turned out to have been tampered with *en route.*'

'*Monsieur!*' Monsieur Pamplemousse raised his eyebrows in mute reproof. He had done no such thing, of course. The food had arrived from Paris early that morning under police escort. It would have taken a braver man than he to have got within ten metres of it under the vigilant eyes of the men from Fauchon. *Défense de toucher* had been the by-word. Only the production of his *Guide* credentials and the fact that Trigaux had taken the opportunity of sending back his pictures in the same consignment had gained him permission to photograph it. They had been right, of course, but as the one responsible for placing the order in the first place, it had been somewhat galling.

Monsieur Pamplemousse shaded his eyes as he looked up at the sky. He reached for his binoculars. The airship seemed to have slowed down over the Baie de Quiberon, almost as though it were treading water.

The Director followed the direction of his gaze. 'No doubt they have slackened speed in order to facilitate pouring the champagne whilst overlooking the oyster-beds; a pleasing touch. We must add it to our press release. What was your final choice?'

'A Gosset '75, *Monsieur*.'

'Ah, the '75! A copybook vintage. A touch austere for some tastes, perhaps, but perfectly balanced. I wonder if they have any at the Hôtel du Port? We can have some over *déjeuner*. I have reserved a table. You look fatigued, Aristide. It will do you good.'

Although he privately doubted if the cellar at the Hôtel du Port would live up to the Director's expectations, Monsieur Pamplemousse was more than happy to fall in with the suggestion.

Organising the meal on the airship had involved him in a non-stop round of telephone calls and other activities. It was only now, with his work virtually at an end, that he suddenly realised just how tired he felt.

'Good! In that case, I suggest we make a move.' The Director rubbed his hands together in anticipation. 'If you follow me we will meet at the Hôtel. No doubt Pommes Frites will be joining us?'

It was a redundant question. Ever alive to the nuances and undertones of conversations going on around him, Pommes Frites was already leading the way. Apart from the stop on the journey down, and the unexpected steak, the trip had not, gastronomically speaking, been a memorable one to date. There had been a lot of talk of food, but very little evidence of it. 'All words and no action' would have been his summing-

118

up had he been stopped in the street by someone conducting a public opinion poll on the state of play to date. Not normally a fish lover (fish was indelibly associated in his mind with cats and therefore hardly worth considering) he had got to the stage when he would have settled for a bowl of *moules à la marinière*, had one come his way. The sight of all the food laid out in the balloon, so near and yet so far away, had been the last straw. Putting food on display and then not eating it was beyond his powers of comprehension.

His disappointment was therefore all the more marked when, some half an hour later, having settled himself comfortably under a table, his taste buds working triple over-time as a result of listening to his master and the Director discussing at length and in savoury detail their forthcoming meal – its preparation, the sauces and other accompanying embellishments – there occurred yet another example of the strange behaviour patterns of human beings which, when they occurred, were hard to credit. The ordering of the food and then the abandonment of a meal before it even arrived was, in his opinion, a prime case in point.

The first Pommes Frites knew of impending disaster was the arrival of a pair of trouser-clad legs at the side of the table and the sound of voices, but his senses told him the new arrival was the bearer of bad news. Had he looked out from under the table-cloth and seen the expression on his master's face as he jumped to his feet his worst fears would have been confirmed.

'Monsieur Pickering!'

'Aristide!'

'I have been looking for you since the day I arrived.'

'On the contrary, you have been avoiding me like the plague.' Mr. Pickering allowed himself a brief, if somewhat enigmatic smile, then immediately became serious again. 'I'm afraid I must ask you to come with me.'

'Both of us?'

There was a moment's hesitation. 'Since it involves the airship, I think, yes.'

119

'Forgive me.' Mr. Pickering turned to the Director. 'I know *of* you, of course, but I haven't had the pleasure of meeting you personally, although . . .' again there was a faint smile, 'that is not entirely true. A matter of paramount importance has come up and we may well be glad of your advice.'

Flattery got him everywhere. The Director was on his feet in a flash; the bib which a moment before had been tied around his neck in readiness for a *plateau de fruits de mer* abandoned along with his napkin.

Pommes Frites heaved a deep sigh as he rose to his feet and followed the others out of the restaurant. He glanced around hopefully as they left, but history did not repeat itself. There were no unattended plates anywhere in sight.

Crossing the road, they headed towards the *Mairie*, then turned down a side street towards the *Gendarmerie*.

Mr. Pickering, having contented himself with generalities on the way, nodded to the duty officer at the desk and led them quickly up some stone stairs to a door on the first floor. Two guards standing in the corridor outside came to attention.

'Excuse me, I shan't keep you a moment.' Mr. Pickering opened the door and disappeared into the room. There was a murmur of voices which stopped abruptly, then the door closed behind him.

The Director drew Monsieur Pamplemousse to one side, out of earshot of the guards. 'Who is this man Pickering?' he hissed. 'What does he want?'

'He helped me once when I was with the *Sûreté, Monsieur*. It concerned a matter affecting security and I was given his name and a London telephone number. He helped me again when I was involved with that girls' finishing school near Evian. He is an expert on many things, but other than that I know little. As for what he wants . . .' Monsieur Pamplemousse gave a non-committal shrug.

He could have hazarded a guess; the uneasy feeling he'd woken with that morning had returned in earnest, but he was

saved the trouble. The door opened and Mr. Pickering beck-
oned them in.

The room was small but crowded. Heads turned as they
entered, then swivelled back towards a man at the far end. He
was standing in front of a blackboard to which a large-scale
map of the area was pinned.

Monsieur Pamplemousse settled himself on a chair between
Mr. Pickering and the Director, then concentrated his attention on what was going on. Without even seeing the faces of
those already present he could have pin-pointed their rank
and status. Just in front of him were two representatives of
government; from the cut of their clothes he guessed they
were products of one of the élite *Grandes Ecoles*, members of
les Grands Corps de l'Etat.

In the first row he picked out the local Prefect of Police.
There was an army major alongside him. Behind them came a
sprinkling of British – he'd seen them grouped under the
Union Jack at the launch – they were probably from the Paris
Embassy. The third row were mainly military. All the occupants of the room had one thing in common; they all looked
tense.

'*Messieurs*, for the benefit of those who have just joined us
I will repeat what I have just told you.'

The speaker was short and stocky, but without an ounce of
fat. He had to be a *Barbouze* – a member of the Special
Police. His face was tanned and leathery. His hair was crew-
cut; his eyes light blue and totally expressionless. Not a good
man to cross, or to be interrogated by, particularly in a closed
room. Monsieur Pamplemousse had met his sort before.
After the Algerian army revolt in November 1964 had been
ruthlessly stamped on by de Gaulle, some of them had started
to show their faces in Paris.

When he spoke it was with an economy of words. It was
hard to tell whether he was put out at being interrupted or
not.

'At eleven ten hours this morning a message was received
by telephone at this station.

121

'I will not bother to read it to you again in full. In essence it said that a bomb is hidden on board the airship. It enumerated certain demands – the release of six Iranian terrorists at present being held in France, plus a considerable sum of money. Unless these demands are met in full by 8.30 this evening the bomb will be detonated. There is no way of communicating with the sender of the message other than by public broadcast, and there was no suggestion that he would be in touch a second time. The message was signed Andreas.'

'Could it be a hoax?' It was the Prefect of Police speaking.

'It could be, but we have reason to believe not. Until we know otherwise we have to treat it as being serious. Deadly serious.' He nodded towards a colleague in the front row. The second man rose to his feet.

'As I am sure most of you will recall, Andreas is a known terrorist who was active up until a few years ago when the pace got too hot for him and he literally vanished from the scene. We believe the message to be genuine because whoever telephoned used a code name which was established at the height of his activities so that both sides always knew whom they were talking to. He is a loner and utterly ruthless. He has never failed to carry out any threats he has ever made.' Again there was a nod and the ball was passed to a third man.

'If it is Andreas, we are not dealing with a time fuse and old-fashioned explosive situation. We are probably dealing with a sophisticated device triggered off by radio. He is a one-time associate of a Jordanian named Abu Ibrahim – a garage mechanic who turned his talents to designing high-tech detonating devices. Ibrahim has since died of cancer, but it was he who manufactured the suitcase bomb which was found on the El Al plane in 1983. That had a double detonating mechanism and used a plastic explosive called Semtex H. At the time it was established that he had made five such suitcases. Only three were ever located, so somewhere in the world there are still two more.'

'The type of explosive is immaterial.' The *Barbouze* showed the first flicker of impatience. 'The important question is does it exist, and if so, what do we do about it?' The second man broke in. 'The whole airship was gone over with a fine-tooth comb this morning. Sniffer-dogs, X-ray equipment, the lot. I would stake my reputation that it was clean.'

'My point,' said his colleague, 'is that Semtex H is virtually invisible by X-ray. And if it was hidden amongst any of the mechanical parts of the wiring of the dirigible the same could be said about the detonating apparatus.'

'Then we cannot afford to take the risk. If it is Andreas he will be deadly serious. He is too old a hand to play at practical jokes. Besides, his reputation will be at stake. He is a professional and he is well paid for his work.'

'What are the possibilities of the demands being met?'

'None whatsoever. Both parties are agreed on that.'

'We are, of course, making "arrangements", but purely as a precautionary measure in case there is a last-minute change of heart.'

'Our Leaderene would never permit it.' One of the British contingent spoke for the first time. 'It would be against all her principles.'

'What are the chances of mounting a rescue attempt? A boarding party by means of a helicopter?'

'Zero.'

The questions started coming thick and fast and were answered with equal speed.

'Commander Winters and Capitaine Leflaix are carrying out a minute search of all the possible areas inside the airship – the ones that are accessible to them that is – but the chances of their finding anything are small.'

'How long can the airship stay up?'

One of the British party rose. 'Long enough. It has loiter facilities.'

'And if the bomb goes off?'

'That depends on where it is. The differential pressure between the inside of the fabric and the outside is quite small. The fabric is laminated polyester and the airship can remain airborne for a long time with a hole in it something like the

123

size of a saucer, but if it has a large tear, that's a different matter. If the bomb is hidden somewhere on the gondola . . .'

The rest was left to the imagination.

'What if the airship returns to base?' It was the Prefect of Police again.

'The instructions are that it is to stay exactly where it is. Any movement will result in the immediate detonation of the device. So far we have managed to keep the press out of it, but it is only a matter of time before they start asking questions. The dirigible containing the heads of state of both France and England is at present stationary over the Golfe du Morbihan. I need hardly tell you of the possible repercussions if the threat is carried out.'

He turned to the map. 'The implication of the last instruction is that Andreas is in a position where he can keep a constant eye on the airship. That would also accord with the use of a very high frequency radio device which ideally needs to be free of anything which would interfere with the path of the signal. Taking a semi-circular field radiating out from the airship, my guess is that it will be located somewhere in this area.'

He ran his finger round the lower half of the map from La Baule in the south-west to Auray in the north-east.

'But that is an impossible task. We shall never search an area that size in time.' It was someone else in the front row, who received a quick rebuff.

'*Impossible*?' Clearly it was not a word in the *Barbouze*'s vocabulary. 'If we start saying things are *impossible* we might just as well all go home!

'A unit of the 11th Parachute Division based at Tarbes is being flown in. When they arrive,' he looked at his watch, 'which will be in approximately two hours from now, they will be deployed on all roads leading into and out of the area and we shall then be in a position to seal it off at a moment's notice.

'A flotilla of French Navy power boats is on its way from St. Nazaire ready to carry out a search for survivors should the worst happen; a submarine will be joining them.'

Monsieur Pamplemousse was impressed. Given the short time at his disposal the *Barbouze* had worked incredibly fast. He must be in a position to exercise considerable authority.

'*Mon Dieu!*' The Director had a sudden thought. He nudged Monsieur Pamplemousse. 'If the airship is blown up,' he whispered, 'the oyster-beds of Locmariaquer will be devastated. The force of the explosion could well dislodge the baby ones from their tiles.'

'The oyster-beds of Locmariaquer will be the least of the problems, *Monsieur*,' said the man coldly. Long exposure to the North African sun had not impaired his hearing.

Conscious of a sudden chill in the atmosphere as heads turned in their direction, Monsieur Pamplemousse rose to his feet.

'May I ask a question? Why 8.30 this evening?'

'Presumably because it will be getting dark by then. Andreas will not wish to lose sight of the airship in case we try moving it under cover of darkness.'

'But the weather is good – there is a full moon. Why not nine o'clock or even midnight?'

There was a pause. '*Monsieur*, if you know of something, either you or your – *associates* . . .' the stress was on the last word.

Monsieur Pamplemousse was about to reply when he felt a restraining touch on his arm and Mr. Pickering rose to his feet.

'*Monsieur*, I must congratulate you on your analysis of the situation. I need hardly add that the resources of Her Majesty's government are available should you require them.'

The pause this time was even longer. The reply when it came was directed at the other occupants of the room, but the eyes remained fixed on Mr. Pickering. 'I understand we also have at our disposal a party of "nuns" who happen to be attending a seminar in Port St. Augustin at this time. Am I correct?'

Mr. Pickering returned the other's stare with equanimity.

'That is so, *Monsieur*.' He fingered his right ear reflectively. 'I think I can safely say they belong to the only order in the world who are able to claim anti-terrorist capability. I repeat, *Monsieur*, they are at your disposal should you have need of them.'

8

Death by Misadventure

'In *Angleterre*,' said Mr. Pickering, 'I know a man who saws Rolls-Royce cars in half.'

'He must be one of two things,' said Monsieur Pamplemousse. 'He must either have extremely strong nerves or be unforgivably foolish.'

'He is neither,' said Mr. Pickering. 'He just happens to be very proficient with a hacksaw. He makes a good living out of welding an extra piece of bodywork in the middle and selling the "stretched" version to Arabs with large families and garages to match.'

The Director looked out of his depth. 'I fail to see what that has to do with our present problem.'

'The point I am trying to make,' said Mr. Pickering, 'is that things are not always what they seem.

'The *Barbouze* is a good man. I have a great deal of respect for him. I'm sure he is first rate at his job. But he is in command and he does not like me.'

'With respect,' said Monsieur Pamplemousse, 'I think it is not so much you he dislikes, it is the circumstances of your being here. It is a question of territories. I doubt if he likes anyone very much, particularly if he thinks they are getting in his way. He is probably a very tidy man with a mind to match.'

Mr. Pickering acknowledged the point. 'I fully understand. I would feel exactly the same way if the positions were reversed. Nevertheless, be that as it may, I – or rather *we*, are here – albeit under sufferance, and if our direct involvement is an embarrassment, then we must go it alone. I, also, have my instructions.' He turned to the Director.

'I must apologise, *Monsieur*, if I have placed you in an awkward situation because of our withdrawal from the briefing, but it seemed to me there was nothing more to be learned, and there are likely to be too many voices raised, too many egos to be satisfied, for the kind of quiet thinking which needs to be done. I will make my peace with the *Barbouze* in due course – we understand each other and we have a common objective – but for the moment at least he will have his work cut out with all the others he has to deal with.'

He turned back to Monsieur Pamplemousse. 'You asked an interesting question just before we left.'

'Why 8.30?'

'Precisely. Why not, as you say, 9 p.m.? There is a natural tendency for people – even terrorists – to go for the round figure.'

Monsieur Pamplemousse weighed the matter carefully in his mind before replying. Other than through telephone calls and one brief meeting in Paris many years before, he scarcely knew Mr. Pickering. Yet his instinct told him he could be trusted. There was an element of mutual respect in their relationship which had been there right from the start. On the other hand, he shuddered to think what might happen if he withheld information from the proper quarters and things went wrong. At least it would earn him a place in history. Instinct won. The truth of the matter was he knew he could say things to Mr. Pickering and they would be accepted without his having to go into a lot of tedious explanations. The same certainly wouldn't be true of those in the other room.

'The circus starts at 9 p.m.,' he said simply.

'Ah!' Mr. Pickering seemed pleased with the answer. 'You

think the two are connected?'

'I didn't until a few minutes ago. Now I am not so sure. There is something very wrong going on there.' Quickly and succinctly he ran through the events to date. The Director remained unusually and commendably silent throughout, only registering faint disappointment when, for the sake of brevity, Monsieur Pamplemousse sped through those areas which he judged could have no possible bearing on the matter under discussion but which, in more ways than one, simply added flesh to the bare bones of his story.

As he got to the end Mr. Pickering felt in his pocket and withdrew a small black and white enprint size photograph. He handed it over without a comment.

It was very grainy and looked like a blow-up from a small section of a larger negative. It was a head and shoulders shot of a man. He wore a black Viva Zapata-style moustache and had black, curly hair. From the angle of his head and the look on his face he appeared to be running away from something or someone. Around his neck there was a gold cross on a chain. Monsieur Pamplemousse placed his hand over the lower half of the picture. The eyes were as he remembered them.

'It is the trapeze artist, Christoph.'

'It is also the only known photograph in existence of Andreas,' said Mr. Pickering. 'It was taken during an incident in Frankfurt some years ago.'

Monsieur Pamplemousse remembered it now. It had been circulated to police forces and immigration offices all over Europe at the time.

'*Mon Dieu!*' The Director jumped to his feet. 'We must inform the authorities at once.'

'The problem with authorities,' said Mr. Pickering slowly, 'is that by definition they tend to act authoritatively, consequently their behaviour pattern tends to be ponderous and is almost always predictable.'

'But if what you say is true,' exclaimed the Director, 'if Christoph and Andreas are one and the same person can he not be arrested? Are you suggesting we should do nothing?' Clearly his involvement in matters outside his normal experience was beginning to worry him.

'No,' said Mr. Pickering, 'I am not. What I am suggesting is that although Andreas may be without mercy, he is certainly not lacking in imagination. He will have planned the whole thing meticulously down to the very last detail over a long period of time and he will have covered every foreseeable eventuality. At the first sign of anything untoward happening he will pull the plugs on the operation without a second's hesitation. If, due to a false move on our part, it is the wrong plug, that could spell disaster for everyone.

'It is abundantly clear that we must discover his whereabouts before 8.30 this evening, and having found him strike before he has a chance to act.' He glanced at his watch. 'That gives us a little over six and a half hours.'

The Director picked up the photograph. 'The man at the meeting was right. It is too big an area to cover in the time available. It will be like looking for a needle in a haystack.'

'The one clear advantage about looking for a needle in a haystack,' said Mr. Pickering, 'is that the one is very different to the other. Besides, I think we can start by eliminating a good deal of the day. If 8.30 is zero hour and the circus starts at 9 p.m., or thereabouts, he must be within half an hour's drive – probably a lot less if he has made allowances for traffic and changing into his costume for the opening parade – say, twenty minutes. That puts it within an area of not more than twelve to fifteen kilometres away. That, in turn, would also fit in with the theory that he needs to be within sight of the airship.'

'Even so . . .' The Director was obviously not entirely convinced. He probably felt his *Légion d'Honneur* was at stake.

'Even so, it is a start.' Mr. Pickering took a yellow Michelin map from his pocket and opened it up. 'It eliminates the whole of the area north of the Vilaine estuary.

'What's the matter, Aristide? You look troubled.'

Monsieur Pamplemousse shrugged. There was still an element about the whole thing that troubled him. 'Is there any reason for this Andreas to go back to the circus? The girl is gone. Presumably he got rid of her because she knew too much and he felt she was about to betray him. If his plan works out and he gets what he wants, he can disappear again. There is nothing to keep him there.'

'If things don't go right,' said Mr. Pickering, 'if something goes violently wrong, his chances of getting away unchallenged will be zero – the whole area will be alive with police and troops. His best bet will be to carry on with his everyday life as though nothing had happened – at least until the first shock-waves die down. As far as he knows there is nothing to link him with the affair. The one person who could have blown his cover is gone. Once the circus moves on and is safely out of Brittany, then he can make himself scarce and we shall be back where we started.

'It has taken a long time to catch up with Mr. Andreas. The present little problem aside, it would be a great misfortune if he slipped through our hands yet again.'

Monsieur Pamplemousse looked at him curiously. Beneath the laid-back manner there was an unexpectedly steely character. In his way, Mr. Pickering would be as tough a nut to crack as the *Barbouze*.

'If it is of any help,' he said, 'I may have some photos of Christoph.' Opening up his case he withdrew the large manila envelope that had arrived with the food that morning, removed a thick batch of glossy black and white enlargements, and spread them out across the table. They were even better than he'd expected. Trigaux had done his stuff as usual. The pictures taken inside the circus tent positively sparkled with life. Apart from a slight graininess, the tight shots of the figure at the top of the trapeze could almost have been taken in a studio.

'Magnificent!' Mr. Pickering's usual aplomb suffered a temporary lapse.

'I trust this is a private arrangement, Pamplemousse,' broke

131

in the Director as he caught sight of *Le Guide*'s logo on the outside of the envelope. 'Otherwise we could have trouble with Madame Grante if she is still on the warpath.'

'I have no idea who Madame Grante might be when she's at home,' said Mr. Pickering mildly, 'but there are plenty of people who would give their eye-teeth to get their hands on these.'

'In that case we must take them next door at once.' The Director tried to reassert his authority. 'After that, I suggest we wash our hands of the whole affair and leave matters to the powers that be. That is what they are there for.'

Mr. Pickering lowered the photographs and began riffling through the remainder on the table. 'I think that would be a great pity, *Monsieur le Directeur*. What do you think, Aristide?'

'Mr. Pickering is right, *Monsieur*. For what it is worth, I will see that copies of the photograph are made available. But as for the rest, I doubt if the *Barbouze* will involve us in his plans. He is interested in facts, not theories. He cannot afford to take chances and play a hunch, whereas we can. Time is not on anyone's side but at least it is worth a try. The worst that can happen is that we are proved wrong.'

'Too many cooks spoil the broth,' said Mr. Pickering, 'and the next room is full of chefs.'

'*Trop de cuisinières gâtent la sauce*.' Monsieur Pamplemousse ventured a translation in case the Director had missed the point, but he needn't have bothered. The culinary allusion had gone home; the parallel was irresistible and capitulation was at hand.

'When did you take these other photographs?' asked Mr. Pickering. He pointed to a series of shots taken from the first reel of film.

Monsieur Pamplemousse thought for a moment. So much had happened since he'd arrived in Port St. Augustin he had almost lost track of time. 'The ones of my car were taken the day I arrived. On the Tuesday.'

'Ah, yes, I heard all about that.' Mr. Pickering looked

embarrassed. 'I'm afraid one of our chaps forgot to "*céder le passage*". Some of your intersections are unbelievably large and complex by our standards. He couldn't stop for fear of their breaking cover.'

Monsieur Pamplemousse wondered what story had been concocted by Mr. Pickering's 'chaps' to cover their escapade. By no stretch of the imagination could the intersection where the accident had taken place have been described as complex – but before he had a chance to enquire further he felt the Director leaning over his shoulder.

'What's this, Pamplemousse? Is that your car lying in the ditch? I trust you have filled in your P81 in triplicate and despatched it to Madame Grante. You know how she is about delay in these matters.'

'Madame Grante again. She sounds even more redoubtable than Andreas. They would make a good pair.' Mr. Pickering sounded distracted. 'It was really these ones of the outside of the circus I was interested in.'

'They were taken on the Wednesday morning. I went along to see if I could get some tickets for the evening performance. I finished off a reel of film so that I could reload before I went up in the airship. Why do you ask?'

Mr. Pickering held up one of the pictures. 'I don't remember seeing a menhir the evening I was there.'

Monsieur Pamplemousse took a closer look. There it was, just as he remembered it that first morning; a large, top-heavy, misshapen, light-grey piece of stone, standing up like a sore thumb. Yasmin's BMW was parked to the right of it, the blue hire-van further away to the left.

Mr. Pickering was right. The menhir hadn't been there that same evening. He'd sensed at the time that there had been an element missing, but it wouldn't have occurred to him in a million years that something so outwardly solid could vanish, although seeing it again made him want to kick himself.

'But it isn't possible. It must have weighed a hundred tons or more. It is as solid as a . . .

'*Ça y est, j'ai compris!*' The penny dropped. Suddenly

everything fell into place at once; the roll of material in the boot of Yasmin's car, the smell of acetone, the bag of light grey powder he'd found in the waste-bin – it must have been filler powder to go with the resin, the paint, the half dry brushes, the piece of sawn-off material he had come across lying on the ground, the pieces of wire and the solder.

A fibreglass menhir! It was on the face of it a preposterous idea, but the more he thought about it the more logical it seemed. As quickly and as briefly as possible he outlined his thoughts. 'It would be an ideal hiding-place. The whole area is so full of stones no one's going to notice an extra one – or if they do they're not going to report it until it is too late.'

Mr. Pickering accepted the thesis without question. 'How many menhirs do you reckon are around here?'

'How many? Probably as many as there are cafés in Paris. This part of Brittany is full of them.'

'If you wanted to erect an artificial one, where would be the best place?'

'If you went somewhere like Carnac you would have the advantage of it being one of many – it could be slipped into one of the great *alignements* – there is one which has over a thousand stones. On the other hand, Carnac is full of tourists – especially at this time of the year when the coach parties start to arrive. It would be much too public and the place is crawling with sightseers and guides and people who know the area like the back of their hand. Besides, we have already decided it has to be nearer than that.'

He paused and gazed out of the window. On the other side of the narrow street a man in shirt sleeves was working at a desk. A woman came into the room carrying a piece of paper which she gave to the man before leaving the room again. He didn't even bother looking up.

'If you simply put it in a field you would be up against the fact that anything unusual would be noticed straight away.'

'You are right.' Mr. Pickering joined him. 'It is always the same in the country. You can get away with murder in a big city, but in the country the slightest change is noticed. My guess would be in the marshes behind La Baule – the Grande Brière. It is still relatively uninhabited. An inhospitable part of the world; full of strange corners where no one goes; also the *Briérons* are fiercely independent. They keep themselves very much apart. It might be several days before anyone bothered to report something out of the ordinary.'

The Director broke in. 'If this Andreas person is in the Grande Brière you will have your work cut out finding him, let alone his plastic menhir. It is worse than the Camargue. Over six thousand hectares of marshland and not a restaurant in sight. Most of it can only be reached by flat-bottomed boat – and then only at those times in the year when the water is high. Have you been there? Poof! You will need a guide!'

'Yes, I have been there on a number of occasions.' Mr. Pickering crossed to the table and opened up the map again. 'You are right about the restaurants, and by its very nature it is not noted for its menhirs either. There is one near Pontchâteau – at a place the English know as "Magdalen Moors", and there is a dolmen – a burial chamber – near Kerbourg. As I recall, those are the only ones Michelin marks, but doubtless there are others less worthy of note. That is what we should be looking for.

'Perhaps we shall have to deal with the *Barbouze* after all. If we get through to Washington it is possible we could get an up-to-date satellite picture of the area. The Americans are taking them all the time and they may well be monitoring this particular operation. A lot of people are interested in diri-gibles these days: NASA, the US Navy, the Coastguards. Airships have a low radar profile on account of the lack of metal. We can get copies faxed over. At least we can eliminate the ones that are marked on the map and something odd may show itself.'

'That will not be necessary.' Monsieur Pamplemousse flipped through the rest of the photographs until he found the section he wanted. 'I did my own aerial survey while I was up in the balloon.'

He cleared a space on the pine-topped table and then

spread the photographs out in sequence; six rows of six. In total they covered the entire Guérande Peninsula to the west, La Baule and the Côte d'Amour to the south and the Parc Régional de Brière to the north and east. Once again the combination of Leica optics and Trigaux's wizardry had not let him down. The enlargements were needle sharp. In places the pictures overlapped more than he would have liked, but it was better that way. At least there were no great gaps.

Mr. Pickering pointed to the second photograph in from the left. It included Port St. Augustin and the circus. 'The menhir has already disappeared.'

'So has the van. Andreas must have got the wind up when the police arrived and started asking questions about Yasmin. He can't have been gone more than about half an hour when I took the picture. That being so . . .' Monsieur Pamplemousse ran his finger over the photographs, following the main road out of Port St. Augustin to the point where it crossed the D774 north of Guérande and then entered the Grande Brière.

They both saw it at the same time, the unmistakable shape of a van parked in a tiny lane leading towards the marshes. To one side there was a small wood and on the western side, facing towards the Baie de Quiberon, there was an area of scrubland dotted with white stones.

Mr. Pickering began counting.

'There are eight menhirs altogether. The question is, which is the odd one out?'

'It may not be any of them. It could still be in the van. There's no sign of anyone about. He may have only just arrived.'

'True. Would you recognise the one we are looking for if you saw it again?'

Monsieur Pamplemousse shook his head. 'I doubt it. There were some markings on the side, but most of them have those anyway. It depends how big the others are. It is impossible to tell from the photograph, but if they are anything like the same size – and presumably he thought of that – then the answer is no – not without getting close to it.'

'That's too risky. Andreas already knows what you look like, and if he's inside already . . .'

Monsieur Pamplemousse suddenly remembered the feeling he'd had that first morning, the feeling of being watched. It was conceivable that Andreas had been inside the menhir even then. No wonder Pommes Frites had behaved the way he had.

'Presumably any kind of spy-hole he has will be facing towards the airship. We might be able to come up from behind.'

Mr. Pickering shook his head. 'It's still too risky. Unless . . .' He crossed over to the window again and stood looking out. After a moment Monsieur Pamplemousse joined him. Nothing had changed. The man in the building opposite was still working away at his desk. He wondered how he would react if he knew what was happening on the other side of the street.

'What springs to mind when you think of *Bretagne*, Aristide?' said Mr. Pickering. 'Apart from menhirs and dolmens, that is.'

'Weather,' said Monsieur Pamplemousse. '*Crêperies*, cider, shellfish, rocky coasts, Muscadet, granite walls, blue roof tiles, narrow streets, fields of artichokes, thatched cottages, onion-sellers from Finistère, lace head-dresses, Tristan and Isolde, Abélard and Héloïse.' He glanced along the street. 'Churches . . .'

'Carry on. You're getting warm.'

'Saints, festivals, calvaries, pardons . . .'

'Exactly.' Mr. Pickering rubbed his hands with pleasure. 'Pardons. I think it is high time we held one of our own. My chaps are dying for a spot of action.'

'Now look here,' the Director, who had remained silent for longer than Monsieur Pamplemousse could remember, was unable to contain himself a moment longer. He rose to his feet. 'Enough is enough. If, as you suggest, this terrorist is concealed inside a menhir – and listening to the various arguments you have put forward, bizarre though the thought might appear to be at first sight, it does seem to be a distinct possibility – then we cannot keep the facts to ourselves. The responsibility must be shared.'

'And what decisions will those we share it with come to?' asked Mr. Pickering mildly. 'Bring in the tanks? Drop a bomb on it? Either will run the risk of triggering off a panic action which will be self-defeating. Our only hope is to use the weapon of surprise. A procession of nuns walking across a field is not an unusual sight in Brittany. There is a religious festival of one kind or another going on practically every day at this time of the year. My chaps have been in the area for a week now and no one has so much as raised an eyebrow. If Andreas does see them it will scarcely register, giving us time enough to move in on him before he has a chance to do anything.'

'And how will we know which menhir he is in?' The Director remained unconvinced. 'Are you going to rush each and every one in turn? What happens to your weapon of surprise if he happens to be in the last one?'

'There are such things as thermal imagers,' said Mr. Pickering. 'They are used for detecting body heat. We can probably arrange to get one through the local fire-brigade.'

Monsieur Pamplemousse sighed. Thermal imagers; fax machines; satellites; dirigibles with low radar profile and hover capability; he sometimes felt as if one day the whole world would collapse under the weight of its own technology. Speaking for himself, he much preferred to entrust his fate and those of others to old-fashioned, tried and tested methods. In his experience they rarely let you down.

Opening up *Le Guide*'s case once again, Monsieur Pamplemousse removed a small tube of ointment. 'I think,' he said, 'I can suggest an even simpler solution to the problem.'

As he caught sight of the object in his master's hand, Pommes Frites rose to his feet, stretched himself, and stood waiting patiently for the next command. The smell of the ointment was one he was unlikely to forget in a hurry. An instinct, born not only out of many hours of unselfish devotion to the cause of duty, but also from encounters too numerous to mention and largely unrecorded save in the stark prose reserved for the annals of the Paris *Sûreté*, told him that his moment of glory was nigh.

Working on the principle that some achieve greatness through sheer hard work and perseverance, whilst others have it thrust upon them, he sensed that after a long period when his talents had gone unappreciated, he was now onto a winning streak. It was only a matter of time before he received his just rewards.

'Will he be all right, Aristide?' The Director peered anxiously through a gap in the trees.

'Pommes Frites?'

'It would be terrible if anything happened. Things would never be the same. His flag is always alongside yours in the operations room.'

Monsieur Pamplemousse gave a start. The operations room at *Le Guide*'s headquarters was a holy of holies. Entry without prior permission was strictly *Interdite*. The position of each and every Inspector at any given moment was marked by a flag on a large map, and kept under constant review by a team of uniformed girls working in shifts. It had never occurred to him that Pommes Frites had his own flag too.

'He is well able to look after himself.'

Monsieur Pamplemousse spoke with rather more confidence than he felt. Privately, he was beginning to wish he'd let Mr. Pickering stick to his original plan of using a thermal imager. It was always the same when it came down to it. Total obedience also meant total trust. You trained an animal to obey your every command and then took advantage of it. He would sooner have gone out there himself than let anything happen to Pommes Frites. He would have loved to have told him so before they set off, but then perhaps he knew.

He watched as Pommes Frites reached the first menhir on the far side of the field, crawling on his stomach and taking advantage of every patch of heather and gorse. He sniffed it and having immediately rejected it, set off towards the next one.

It must have been the same way with Yasmin. Despite everything, when she climbed up onto the trapeze that night she must still have had total trust in her partner, otherwise she couldn't have done it. And yet, on the other side of the coin, it could be argued that she had been about to betray Andreas. Morally, she would have been right to do so, but in terms of human relationships she must have gone through agonies of doubt. The difference between her and Pommes Frites was that in no way would it have crossed his mind to betray his master. The thought didn't make Monsieur Pamplemousse feel any better.

Another menhir, nestling amongst a mass of hollyhocks, was tested and found wanting. Monsieur Pamplemousse instinctively drew back as Pommes Frites moved nearer to his hiding place in the bushes.

He looked around. If anyone had said to him a few days earlier that the following week would find both him and the Director crouched in a *Bretagne* wood dressed as nuns, he would have laughed his head off. Life had strange and unexpected twists. Doucette would be appalled if she could see him. She was probably worried enough as it was, for he still hadn't sent his postcard.

Behind him some twenty or so robed figures crouched in the undergrowth, their tense faces buried between the huge wings of their *coiffes*. He wondered what they had concealed beneath their habits – stun grenades, Browning 9mm pistols, Heckler and Koch 9mm sub-machine guns probably. They were the favourite weapons. Anyone stumbling across them unexpectedly while on a nature ramble would be in for a rude surprise.

High above on the far side of the scrubland off to his right he could see the stationary airship, a speck in the distant sky. He wondered if those aboard had enjoyed their lunch. Enjoyed wouldn't be exactly the right word in the circumstances, but it would be a pity if they had let it go to waste and it would have helped pass an hour or so. Time must be hanging very heavily by now. At least the weather was good. He didn't care to dwell on how they would have felt if it had been as bad as on the day he had gone up.

Monsieur Pamplemousse felt someone nudge him on his other side. 'Third time lucky!' Mr. Pickering pointed towards a menhir some halfway across the scrub. Pommes Frites was lying alongside it wagging his tail. He was too well trained to look their way. Instead, he slithered backwards along the ground, never for a second taking his eyes off his quarry until he reached the safety of a patch of taller shrubs.

'Here we go!' Mr. Pickering moved away and held a brief conversation with one of the nuns. In response to a hand signal the rest of them rose quietly to their feet and formed themselves into a line two abreast. A moment later, as they set off along a path through the wood which took them to a point somewhere behind the menhir, something which had been bothering Monsieur Pamplemousse ever since they had arrived on the scene crystallised in his mind. There was no sign of a vehicle parked anywhere nearby; neither the blue van nor Yasmin's car. If Andreas was planning a quick getaway it didn't make sense. He could have kicked himself for not thinking of it before, but it was too late to do anything about it. The crocodile of nuns was already emerging through a gap in the trees. Heads bowed, hands clasped in front of them, they made their way slowly but inexorably across the scrubland in a direction which would take them past the menhir. Another ten or twelve paces and the leaders would be level with it.

There was a movement in the undergrowth and Pommes Frites was back. Without taking his eyes off the scene, Monsieur Pamplemousse reached out and gave him a congratulatory pat. The hair on his neck felt stiff. He was still tense, ready to spring into action at a moment's notice.

In the event it wasn't needed. It was all over in a matter of seconds. Although seeing it all unfold before him it felt

almost as though he was watching a carefully rehearsed television drama being replayed in slow motion.

Without a word being uttered, the whole column suddenly
threw themselves on the ground. A moment later the menhir
rocked under a hail of fire. As the echo of the shots died away
two of the nuns jumped to their feet and rushed to either side
of it, machine guns at the ready. A door swung open and
hung drunkenly on its hinges.

For a brief moment no one moved, then there came the
sound of a distant explosion. Instinctively everyone turned
and looked towards the sea.

'Jesus!' Mr. Pickering crossed himself. 'I don't believe it!'

9

DINNER WITH THE DIRECTOR

Mr. Pickering removed a bottle of white wine from a large silver bucket alongside the table and poured a little of the contents into his glass. He swirled it round deftly and expertly, then held the glass to his nose. 'I think we'll dispense with the services of the waitress,' he said. 'I don't know about you, but I'm dying for a drink.'

After displaying the label for Monsieur Pamplemousse and the Director to inspect, he filled the rest of the glasses and replaced the bottle alongside its twin in the ice-bucket.

'A Coulée-de-Serrant. It is from the estate of a certain Madame Joly. They're not easy to find. Even in a good year only a small quantity is made and most are drunk far too young. I happened to come across three bottles in a little wine shop in Nantes soon after I arrived. I'm afraid these are the last two.'

'In that case,' said the Director, 'we are very privileged.'

Mr. Pickering looked pleased. 'It is a wine with an interesting history. The first vines in Anjou were planted by monks in the twelfth century.'

Monsieur Pamplemousse tested the bouquet. There was a familiar scent of honeysuckle. 'I remember your first bottle,' he said. 'It was discarded by an old *sorcière* outside the Hôtel du Port.'

143

'Ah, yes.' Mr. Pickering didn't bat an eyelid. 'The harridan. You resisted her attentions manfully. Madame Pamplemousse would have been proud of you, I'm sure.

'I couldn't believe my eyes when I saw you coming towards me that first night. Having had reports from Interpol of Andreas being somewhere in the area, the last thing I wanted was to be seen talking to an ex-member of the *Sûreté*. He might not have known who you were, but I couldn't afford to take the risk. We didn't know at the time that he was with the circus.'

'You chose a good disguise,' said Monsieur Pamplemousse. 'I doubt if anyone would have come within a mile of you.'

'That's what I thought, but you'd be surprised,' said Mr. Pickering cryptically. He shrugged the matter off. 'I fear I am a frustrated actor at heart and like all actors I get the occasional kick out of being someone else. At school I was known for a while as "The Scarlet Pimple".

'Wine happens to be my other weakness. That's why I could never have become an Olivier. Olivier would have drunk methylated spirits if it enabled him to get inside the character of the old woman.'

Monsieur Pamplemousse was tempted to say Olivier would have chosen a cheaper after-shave as well, but that would have sounded too much like a put-down. Instead, he lifted his glass and smelt the bouquet. Then he sipped a little of the wine and let it flow over his palate. It was flinty-dry and aromatic with the taste of wild flowers. An exceptional wine by any standards. He raised his glass.

'*A votre santé*, Mr. Pickering!'

'Your very good health!'

'Congratulations to you both on a successful mission.' The Director joined them in clinking glasses.

Monsieur Pamplemousse was conscious of eyes watching them from other tables in the Ty Coz's dining room. The sight of two nuns and a Mother Superior arriving with their own wine and imbibing it with such obvious enjoyment probably confirmed the worst suspicions of many of those present.

Mr. Pickering looked at his watch. 'The airship must have crossed the English coast by now. Their journey will be nearly at an end.'

'I still find it hard to believe,' said the Director. 'I have to confess that when I heard the explosion I thought my worst fears had been realised. I fully expected to see the dirigible coming down in flames.'

'You were not alone,' said Mr. Pickering.

Monsieur Pamplemousse inwardly voiced his agreement. It had been a nasty moment, one he wouldn't wish to repeat in a hurry. 'And the caravan?'

'Almost totally wrecked. One side has completely disappeared. Andreas ended up as a kit of parts for someone the world is well rid of.'

'There were no other casualties?'

'None, fortunately. If it had happened later in the evening when everyone was arriving for the circus it could have been a disaster area.'

'But why? I still do not understand why.' The Director pointedly made play with his empty glass. 'Did he have more explosive stored there? If so, what caused it to go off?'

Monsieur Pamplemousse exchanged a quick glance with Mr. Pickering and received the go-ahead.

'I think, *Monsieur*, it was partly to do with fate and partly to do with Pommes Frites.'

'A formidable combination.' Mr. Pickering took the hint and reached across the table in order to recharge the Director's glass. 'A case of the proverbial irresistible force teaming up with an immovable object.'

'Pommes Frites found the explosive in the first place. He picked up the scent the day I travelled on the airship. It was hidden in one of the bags of ballast.' Monsieur Pamplemousse reached down and felt under the table for the subject under discussion. He received an affectionate lick in return. 'One tends to forget that he is a dog of many talents. Long before he and I met he attended a sniffer course in Paris. I understand he was top of his class for that year. He won the Pierre Armand trophy.

'Fate then stepped in and decreed that I put the bag in the waste bin outside Andreas's caravan.'

Fate, or was it pre-ordained? If it was the latter, then it had been operating from the moment his car ended up in a ditch the day he arrived, perhaps even before that. It was an interesting point. On the same basis, the fate of two leading heads of state in the western world had been largely determined by his spearing the end of Pommes Frites' nose with a ball-point pen. It was a sobering thought. The manufacturers would probably love to be able to quote the fact in their literature.

He looked around the room. Strange unidentifiable agricultural implements adorned the walls; the whole area surrounding the huge stone fireplace was taken up with an unlikely mural of the Camargue. Wild horses were dashing towards the exit – probably trying to escape the ghastly food at the Ty Coz. He couldn't for the life of him understand why the Director had insisted on dining there in the first place.

Sitting at a nearby table was a young English family; mother, father and three children, all red from the sun and wind. The children kept looking across and giggling. A scattering of Germans and a few French families, very casually dressed, were eating noisily; the prime window seat was occupied by an elderly English couple – probably the Bentley owners. They looked as if they owned the table as well. The man was wearing a cravat, his one concession to their being on holiday. He would probably dress for dinner even if they were in the middle of the African jungle, resolutely refusing to 'go native'. A young couple, both wearing headphones, jiggled to different rhythms over a bowl of *moules*. Perhaps everyone was taking part in some pre-ordained plan. Given the abysmal food, he couldn't picture any other reason. What *had* they all done to deserve such a fate? The strangest part of all was the fact that they actually seemed to be enjoying themselves. It made a mockery of his job with *Le Guide*.

'I was explaining to *Monsieur le Directeur*,' Mr. Pickering broke into his reverie, 'the one thing we hadn't bargained for was Andreas not actually being inside the artificial menhir, but simply using it as a relay station. The main control for detonating the explosive was safely inside the caravan. Given his background and knowledge of electronics it wasn't a difficult thing to set up. It turned the whole thing into an arm's-length transaction as it were, and it also had the advantage that he could keep an eye on the airship from his window and give himself an alibi at the same time if things went wrong. No doubt when the experts search the wreckage of the caravan they will find all the evidence, but he must have had some warning device to let him know if the menhir was being tampered with. As soon as that sounded he took the decision to blow up the airship and in doing so blew himself up instead. It was, in many ways, not unjust, even an elegant solution to many people's problems.'

The Director broke in. 'But how did he manage to get the explosive on board the airship in the first place?'

'It probably wasn't all that difficult. As Aristide will tell you, security was fairly lax in the beginning. All he would have had to do was turn up carrying a brief-case and clip-board. You can go anywhere if you carry a clip-board.'

Mr. Pickering was saved any further explanations by the arrival of his first course: *coquilles St. Jacques* – cooked the Breton way, in cider. The Director had chosen the sea-food platter which arrived on a vast oval tray placed on a stand in the centre of the table. On a bed of crushed ice lay a montage of winkles and mussels, baby shrimps, oysters, pink *langoustines*, crabs and other delicacies, nestling amongst dark green sea-weed and yellow halves of a lemon.

On the grounds that it might have been bought outside rather than made in the Ty Coz's kitchen, Monsieur Pamplemousse had ordered a portion of pork *rillettes*. It looked rather lonely on its over-large plate. Glancing at the other dishes, he almost regretted his choice, but it was a case of being better safe than sorry.

A large *faux-filet* steak, already partly cut-up, arrived in a separate dish and was placed on the floor beside his feet. Pommes Frites eyed it non-committally from beneath the table-cloth. Like his master, he had his doubts.

As the waitress wished them '*bon appétit*' and withdrew, the Director tucked a napkin into his shirt collar and helped himself to a shrimp. 'Explosives, sabotage, hijackings, terrorism, fibreglass menhirs . . . what *is* the world coming to?'

'What indeed?' said Mr. Pickering. 'Mind you, I may go into business manufacturing fibreglass menhirs myself when I retire. I'm sure there are lots of people in England who would like one at the bottom of their garden. They would make very good sheds – or homes for gnomes.'

'There must be many people in Brittany,' said Monsieur Pamplemousse, 'who wish they *hadn't* got one in their garden.'

'The grass is always greener on the other side of the fence.' Mr. Pickering reached for the second bottle of wine. Under cover of the sea-food platter the Director surreptitiously drained his glass and applied a napkin to his mouth.

'I congratulate you on your choice, Pickering. I must make a note of the vineyard. The wine has an uncommon potency.'

Mr. Pickering acknowledged the compliment. 'It is an anomaly of your otherwise excellent French wine laws. When the *appellation* was first created the vineyards mostly produced a sweet white wine so they were allowed only a very small yield per hectare and the alcoholic content had to be a minimum of 12.5 degrees. Although many of them have now turned to making a much drier wine they still have to retain the same high degree of alcohol. It is a handicap to the growers, but an enormous bonus for the rest of us . . .' He broke off as a series of bleeps sounded from somewhere under his scapular. 'Please excuse me. I think I am needed. Perhaps, if you catch the eye of the waitress, you could ask for the condiments. That is my only complaint so far – a definite lack of salt in the cooking. It does help to bring out the flavour, you know.'

Monsieur Pamplemousse shook his head as Mr. Pickering disappeared. 'A strange race the British. Their knowledge of wine often exceeds our own, but when it comes to food . . .'

'Perhaps, Aristide, your tastebuds have become jaded over the years by too much good living,' said the Director. 'You have yet to try the *rillettes.*'

Feeling rebuffed from an unexpected corner, Monsieur Pamplemousse broke off a piece of toast, reached for his knife, cut off a wedge of chunky paste, added a gherkin, set his taste buds in motion with a black olive, then sat back to contemplate the result. It was, he had to admit, better than he had expected.

The olive was jet-black and plump; the *rillettes* had clearly been made from prime meat, he could taste goose as well as pork; the gherkin had been pickled in a delicately spiced mixture of wine vinegar and dill.

Hearing a rattling noise at his feet he looked down. Pommes Frites had finished his steak and was licking his lips with relish.

'Well, Aristide?'

'I have tasted worse, *Monsieur.*' His reply was suitably guarded.

'Good. Madame Grante will be pleased.'

'Madame Grante?' Monsieur Pamplemousse paused with another portion of toast halfway to his mouth. A delicately balanced gherkin fell off and landed on the floor. Pommes Frites eyed it with interest. 'What does Madame Grante have to do with it?'

'Ah, Aristide.' The Director regarded him unhappily from behind a pair of nutcrackers which he had been about to apply to a lobster claw. 'I am very glad you asked me that. Very glad indeed.'

Monsieur Pamplemousse waited patiently while the Director busied himself with the inside of the claw. For someone who had professed himself eager to answer a question, he was being somewhat tardy.

'My reasons for suggesting you stayed here, Aristide, were

several-fold.'

'*Several*-fold, *Monsieur*?' Monsieur Pamplemousse eyed the Director suspiciously. 'Are you saying there is another fold to come?'

'That is one way of putting it.' The Director looked, if anything, even more unhappy.

'Madame Grante is a good woman, Aristide, a good woman. Much maligned by other members of staff, but a good woman for all that. However, I fear she took extreme umbrage over my intervention during the little argument you had with her recently concerning your last lot of expenses. Storm clouds were gathering over the Parc du Champ de Mars. In the end for the sake of peace I had to strike a bargain.'

'A bargain, *Monsieur*? I'm afraid I do not entirely understand what you are saying.'

'The Ty Coz, Aristide, belongs to a distant relative of Madame Grante. She approached me some while ago with a view to its being inspected for inclusion in *Le Guide*. I said to her that although she could expect no favoured treatment – which, in fairness, she never sought – I would arrange for an early visit. Then, when she heard you were coming to the area she brought the matter up again, knowing she could rely on your judgement and honesty.'

'The Ty Coz, *Monsieur*? In *Le Guide*?'

The Director helped himself to an *oursin*. 'You feel it is not "Stock Pot" material, Aristide? I have to say this sea-food platter is beyond reproach.'

'Not "Stock Pot" material?' Monsieur Pamplemousse could hardly believe his ears. 'After my experience the other evening I would not recommend it for an *oeuf* saucepan – an *oeuf* saucepan riddled with holes – not even a colander! After the other evening I never want to hear the words *La Cuisine Régionale Naturelle* again.'

'Ah!' The Director visibly brightened. 'That, Aristide, is one wish you may be sure of being granted.'

Monsieur Pamplemousse stared at the Director. 'You mentioned a bargain, *Monsieur*,' he said slowly.

The Director gave a sigh. 'The long and the short of it, Aristide, is that there is no such thing as *La Cuisine Régionale Naturelle*. It was a practical joke on the part of Madame Grante. A figment of her imagination. One which occurred to her soon after she learned you were coming here. She sent word down to her relative and clearly he was only too willing to oblige. You alone were singled out for the so-called *cuisine*.'

'And you agreed to it, *Monsieur*?' Memories of the expression on Madame Grante's face the last time he saw her came flooding back; the look of triumph should have been a warning sign. The bitterest pill of all was the thought that the Director had been in on it too!

'You must understand, Aristide, that I had very little choice. You are not the only one to experience trouble with your P39s. In some ways those working out in the field are fortunate. It is hard to argue with a man who says he needed extra *essence* for his car so that he could circumnavigate a traffic jam in order to reach a restaurant on time. It is his word against Madame Grante's. I have no such advantage.

'Besides, short of committing physical assault on her person in order to retrieve the key, it was the only way I could get my balloon back. And with the Elysée Palace awaiting its return I had no alternative.

'It does show that deep down Madame Grante is not without a sense of humour. A trifle warped, perhaps. But it is there, nevertheless. All is not lost if she has it in her to concoct practical jokes.'

Warped! It was no more a practical joke than that played by Madame Grante's mother when she gave birth to her in the first place. It was more a calculated act of revenge. Monsieur Pamplemousse was about to let forth on the subject when there was a rustle of cloth and Mr. Pickering arrived back. He was carrying a salt-cellar.

'Sorry I was a long time. I went into the *Hommes* by mistake and had to wait until the coast was clear before I could get out again. All very tedious.

'That was our Foreign Office on the phone. It seems the airship has now landed safely. A statement is being issued congratulating all concerned and expressing hopes for the future – the usual thing. For the time being there will be no mention of the attempt to blow it up. They will play that side of it by ear. You will be pleased to know that those in charge of catering arrangements are especially singled out for praise. Both food and wine were judged to be beyond reproach.'

The Director raised his glass. 'I would like to second that, Aristide.'

'Hear, hear.' Mr. Pickering joined in the toast. 'And my own thanks to you both once again for all your help. My men are already on their way home.'

Monsieur Pamplemousse finished off his *rillettes* and came to a decision. He signalled for the waitress.

'With your permission, *Monsieur*, I think I shall change my order.'

'Does that mean,' ventured the Director, 'that you have revised your opinion of the Ty Coz? You think it may be worthy of a mention? A recommendation? A future "Stock Pot", perhaps?'

'We shall have to see, *Monsieur*.' Monsieur Pamplemousse refused to be drawn. 'You would not expect Pommes Frites to judge a restaurant on one steak alone.' He felt an approving movement at his feet.

'You are the judge, Aristide. It is your taste buds that will have to make the ultimate decision. One must not let personal matters affect the outcome.

'However, take care when ordering the dessert. I have arranged for a bottle of Château d'Yquem to be made ready – the 1904. It would be a pity to waste it on something mundane.'

A 1904 Château d'Yquem! Monsieur Pamplemousse could hardly believe his ears. What riches! No wonder the Director had trouble with his P39s. It must have cost a small fortune. Suddenly all was forgiven. If it was a case of quid pro quo, then it was worth every centime. Clearly, by his expression, Mr. Pickering felt the same way.

'I ordered two bottles for the maiden voyage,' explained the Director. 'Afterwards it occurred to me that they might not even get through one and it seemed a pity to waste it. Who knows where it would have ended up?'

'Of course, *Monsieur*. I'm sure Madame Grante will understand.'

'I hope, Pamplemousse,' said the Director severely, 'that Madame Grante will never know.'

'Madame Grante again?' Mr. Pickering pricked up his ears. 'I feel I almost want to meet her.'

'It could be arranged,' said Monsieur Pamplemousse. 'You could travel back to Paris with me tomorrow.'

'Unfortunately,' said Mr. Pickering, 'I'm afraid that won't be possible. I am arranging for Mrs. Pickering to join me for a few days. The sea air will do her good. It will help blow the cobwebs away.'

He glanced around the dining room. 'We could do worse than stay here. Eunice would appreciate the décor. Perhaps you could send me some copies of those photographs you took of the old harridan outside the *Sanisette*. She would appreciate those too.'

It was hard to tell if Mr. Pickering was being serious or not. It was hard to tell a lot of things with Mr. Pickering. The English were trained from an early age not to reveal their true feelings, even when making jokes.

The restaurant was almost empty. Couples with young children had already gone up to their rooms, those without were thinking about it over a final, lingering coffee.

The d'Yquem almost defied description. Rich, fragrant, the colour of old gold, and despite its age, in perfect condition.

At the end of their meal Monsieur Pamplemousse, feeling more replete that he had for a long time, positively awash with good things and with the taste of the Director's wine still lingering in his mouth, announced his intention of taking Pommes Frites for a last stroll down to the harbour.

The Director and Mr. Pickering said their goodbyes in the foyer, then the Director went up to his room to make a telephone call. 'You go ahead, Aristide,' he called. 'I will catch up with you down at the Port.'

Mr. Pickering hesitated as they made their way out of the hotel. He obviously had something on his mind.

'I think you will find the girl from the circus much recovered, Aristide,' he said. 'I'm told you were worried about her.'

'Yasmin? You know her?'

'I know *of* her. When she came round she started calling out your name. I happened to hear about it quite by chance. Ironically, the staff at the hospital kept trying to feed her grapefruit. Having seen you the previous evening it suddenly clicked in my mind.

'When she realised the truth of what had happened she went into a state of shock. That was when she was moved. Luckily for her as it turned out; Andreas might have had another go. Now she is on the mend – it is only a matter of time.'

Monsieur Pamplemousse looked put out. 'Why wasn't I told?'

'I did my best to pass on the news,' said Mr. Pickering, sounding equally aggrieved, 'but you kept avoiding me.'

'*Touché*!' Monsieur Pamplemousse acknowledged defeat gracefully.

'One of the especially nice things about your country, Aristide,' said Mr. Pickering, as he waved goodbye, 'is that you do have exactly the right word for everything.'

It occurred to Monsieur Pamplemousse as he and Pommes Frites made their way down the road that he didn't even know where Mr. Pickering was staying. Perhaps their paths would cross again one day. It was a very small world.

The church clock was striking eleven as they reached the harbour. He led the way down to the narrow strip of beach left by a high tide which was now on the turn. Walking on the dry sand was hard work, and twice he stumbled over a discarded beer can. After a few minutes he gave up and mounted some steps leading to the promenade. The young couple from the hotel strolled past arm in arm, their Walkman sets going full blast. What it must be like on the business end of the headphones was hard to imagine. In a few years' time they would probably both be deaf; not that it would matter very much by the look of it. Strange that an invention which had its roots in communication should be death to all conversation.

The circus was in darkness. Not surprisingly, there could have been no performance that evening. Even before he got there he caught a whiff of charred wood. There was a police car parked near the wreckage. He could see the occasional glow of a cigarette from one of the occupants. For a moment or two he toyed with the idea of crossing the road and knocking on Madame Caoutchouc's door, then he thought better of it. Besides, there was nothing he could say that hadn't been said already, and he didn't want to risk a second attack of cramp. It would be another news item for the local *journal*, which must be having a field day. Perhaps it would be put down to a gas cylinder exploding.

He stood for a while thinking about Yasmin, wondering if he was pleased or sorry not to have seen her perform. Suddenly their meeting seemed an age away.

As he turned to make his way back along the promenade he caught sight of someone standing beside one of the telephone *cabines*. Pommes Frites pricked up his ears and as he ran forward a young girl wearing a thin, white cotton dress came towards them.

'Sister, please may I speak with you?'

Monsieur Pamplemousse looked round, then realised she was talking to him. She had dark, curly hair and an oval, Breton face. Her lipstick looked brown under the artificial light.

'Of course. What is it you want?'

'*Quelle heure est-il?*'

Without thinking, he looked at his watch. 'It is fifteen

minutes past eleven.' The gold Cupillard Rième gleamed momentarily in the light. Patently it was not a ladies' model.

If the girl noticed, she was unperturbed; rather the reverse it seemed, for she immediately fell into step alongside him, assuming an almost proprietorial air. It wouldn't have surprised him if she'd linked arms.

'Would you like to hear about my problems?'

'Your problems?' She looked hardly old enough to have problems, other than with her homework. The promenade was now totally deserted. Even the couple with the earphones were nowhere to be seen. He tried to keep his voice as high as possible.

'Tell me, my dear, what is troubling you?'

The girl lowered her head. 'I am afraid it is to do with men, Sister.'

'Ah, men.' Monsieur Pamplemousse managed to imbue his reply with all the sympathy at his command. His protective instincts were roused. How often had he not heard the same remark. Men! A pretty girl, young and full of innocence, still at school, and yet already at the mercy of all and sundry. Men who wanted nothing more than to use her to satisfy their selfish lusts.

'My child, you must understand that young men are not like young girls. They cannot always help themselves. It is in their nature to be the hunter. Sadly, and it is hard to understand I know, sex is often uppermost in their minds.'

'I know, Sister. It isn't always the young ones who are the worst either.' The girl ran her tongue slowly round her upper lip. Monsieur Pamplemousse did his best to pretend he hadn't noticed. His own lips suddenly felt remarkably dry.

'You must not lose faith, my child,' he began. 'Always remember, true faith needs no evidence.' He wondered where he had heard the phrase before. He was beginning to enjoy his part. Perhaps he had missed his vocation.

'But, Sister, it is not the fault of the men.' The girl stopped and stared up at him through large, round eyes. He couldn't help but notice that in the moonlight they also looked

156

impossibly blue. 'If it was only that there would be no problem. I am well able to look after myself. It is my fault. I think I must have a devil inside me. I cannot leave them alone. I think of little else. It keeps me awake at night.'

'You can't!' Monsieur Pamplemousse lowered his voice. 'I mean, it does?'

'In the long winter months when the nights seem endless and during the summer when they are hot . . .

'It is not just sex either, I mean, ordinary sex. It is . . . other things.'

'*Other* things?' Monsieur Pamplemousse looked round uneasily. Pommes Frites was pointedly relieving himself on a nearby lamp-post. He always seemed to have reserves he could draw on for such occasions. He was wearing his *déjà vu* expression. It was hard to tell whether it had to do with his task in hand or the new arrival. Strongly suspecting the latter, Monsieur Pamplemousse avoided his gaze, listening instead to the complicated tales coming from alongside him. They were growing wilder and more improbable by the minute. How much of it was true and how much a product of the girl's imagination he had no idea, but clearly she had a future in the world of letters. Had he been a literary agent he would have signed her up on the spot.

'My dear,' he exclaimed. 'This is terrible. Have you not made your confession to the good Father?'

'Many times, Sister. But sometimes it seems as though he does not really wish me to be cured. I think he looks forward to my visits. He is always asking me when I am coming next. He is excitable and lately I have become frightened of being in the same box with him. Which is why I have turned to those of your calling.'

Monsieur Pamplemousse looked round uneasily. 'That is what we are here for, my dear.'

She looked up at him again and moved a little closer. 'You nuns have been so good to me, and so generous.'

'We have?' Monsieur Pamplemousse felt his voice going again.

The girl nodded vigorously. 'Yes, all of you. Ever since you arrived. There is not one of you this past week who has not listened to me with patience and understanding, often far into the night. Some of you kept coming back for more. But now that most of you have left I don't know where to turn.'

'My child, my poor child,' Monsieur Pamplemousse looked towards the port. He reached out, intending to point her in that direction, then thought better of it. Allard was right. He always maintained there was one in every class. And he should know – he'd once been a teacher. Some of his tales about sixth-formers asking to stay on after school because they were having trouble with their biology homework were spellbinding.

'Will you listen to me, Sister? There are many more things I can tell you. Your time won't be wasted.'

Monsieur Pamplemousse took a deep breath. He sensed Pommes Frites concentrating on their every word, looking from one to the other as he waited for them to catch up.

Hearing footsteps he glanced across the road. They were heading towards the *Sanisette*. He hesitated, but only for a second. It was too good an opportunity to miss.

'I think,' he pointed towards the approaching figure. 'I think it is really a case for the Mother Superior. She is very wise in such matters. I'm sure she will listen to you.'

'Thank you, Sister. Oh, thank you.' For a moment he thought the girl was going to kiss him, then he realised she had her hand out. He reached automatically into an inside pocket and withdrew a fifty franc note.

A moment later she was gone. It was just as well. It could have been an expensive evening.

Pommes Frites registered his approval with a wag of the tail as he followed his master towards the Quai Général de Gaulle. He wasn't at all sure what had been going on, but he sensed that all was now well again. The crisis had passed.

Apart from a few lights coming from the Hôtel and from some of the yachts at their moorings, the Port was in darkness. Somewhere, far out at sea, there was a flashing beacon.

A fishing boat chugged its way out through the harbour entrance. The men on deck were busy coiling ropes, getting ready for their night's work.

Monsieur Pamplemousse stayed until the light at the masthead was a barely visible speck on the horizon, then he turned and made his way slowly back towards the town. At long last he posted Doucette's card at the P.T.T. – with luck it might even reach Paris before he did. It felt almost like an act of absolution.

He glanced along the narrow street towards the *Gendarmerie*. All the lights on the upper floors were on. The *Barbouze* must still be at it. He could picture the inquests being held. They were likely to be at it all through the night. He was glad to be out of it.

'Pamplemousse! Pamplemousse!' He heard a pounding of feet and a figure suddenly loomed out of the darkness behind them. It was the Director. He was clutching his wallet. It crossed Monsieur Pamplemousse's mind that perhaps he wanted change for a 200 franc note, then he dismissed the idea as being unworthy. The Director looked as if he was in need of help of a different kind. His habit was not at its best. At a passing-out parade in the Vatican he would not have been in line for the golden sceptre as the best turned out Mother Superior of his year. He was also patently short of breath.

'Thank goodness you're still here. You will never believe what I have to tell you.'

Monsieur Pamplemousse looked at the Director. He thought of the time that he and Pommes Frites had spent in Port St. Augustin; he thought of Mr. Pickering, the dirigible, and those who had travelled in it; he thought of the circus, of Madame Caoutchouc and of Andreas; he thought of Yasmin and the fact that tomorrow he would be able to stop off at the hospital and see her again. Then he looked up. The sky was inky-black. He could see the Milky Way and the Plough and beyond that the North Star. Glinting faintly above him were the Great Bear and a host of other heavenly bodies of greater and lesser magnitude.

'*Monsieur*,' he said innocently, 'on such a night as this anything is possible. Tell me the worst.'